THINKING THROUGH TO THE OTHER SIDE

Thinking Through to the Other Side

A Memoir of India

LYNN LITTERINE

Marc Kaufman

Transition

In 1987, my journalist husband, Marc, and I took our 6-year-old and 15-month-old sons to India for three years. I left a twin house in Chestnut Hill, a pleasant neighborhood in the northwest corner of Philadelphia. I left longtime friends. I left reliable electricity. I left water that was safe to drink from the tap. I left a nearby Toys 'R' Us that was the size of a football field. I left produce that didn't have to be sterilized. I left disposable diapers. I left hamburgers. I left Ben & Jerry's ice cream. We spent 18 hours in planes and airports traveling 7,597 miles from New York to New Delhi. There, I moved into a house with servants' quarters and servants in those quarters. I made new friends. I dealt with wildly inconsistent electricity. I drank water that was first boiled in an aluminum kettle the size of a holiday turkey and then filtered through ceramic. I shopped for toys at a market stall and came home with huge rubber balloons and a clay crocodile ("Look, boys! It's Lyle!") for my unimpressed sons. I diapered my toddler in cloth that his *ayah* (nanny) pounded clean on the marble floor of our guest-room shower. I ate water buffalo lasagna and rose petal ice cream.

For three years, I tried to understand what was going on around me. Sometimes I made sense of India, and sometimes I made no sense of India at all. What follows is about my life as "Mom" to two small boys, as "Madame" to nine full- and part-time servants, and as one of "the foreigners" whose presence the New Delhi police checked on several times a year. I wanted an adventure; an adventure is what I got. As Marc predicted when he first went over to India alone, "Another thing becoming clear to me is that this is going to be a real eye-opening and soul-deepening experience for me and us."

I begin at the beginning …

Arrival

Indira Gandhi International Airport was like no other airport I'd been in. The mess from new construction was familiar, but having people—men, women, and children—wrapped in quilts and sleeping on the corridor floors was not. The hour was 2 a.m., and despite the bright terminal lights, they slept on.

"Who are they?" I asked my husband, who'd already spent three months in India.

"The construction workers," he said. "They live with their families where they work."

International flights always landed in Delhi during the night, and all my subsequent arrivals would have a surreal feeling, but not one was ever as surreal as the first. For most of the long flight from Amsterdam, the only light below our plane came from lightning flashes that revealed jagged peaks; few cities or towns lit up the darkness below. In the terminal, I'd moved from the flight's dark dream into an illuminated one where babies slept on the airport floor. I couldn't imagine more meagre lodgings, but India would stretch my imagination over and over again.

The terminal had no air conditioning and was stifling. June in India before the monsoon arrives routinely brings temperatures in the high 90s with no humidity. Marc asks me now, "Don't you remember the body heat from all those people in the terminal?" What I do remember instead was the rich odor of human sweat. In dry-season heat, even at night, the body sweats to stay alive.

Outside the terminal, the ambient smell shifted from sweat to something herbal and smoky. Back in the States, I would have guessed it was marijuana smoke.

"Burning cow dung," Marc said.

Out among the rapeseed fields that surrounded the airport, the darkness held a few winking flames. Earlier, farmer's families had cooked dinner over fires fueled by dried cow dung. The fires were dying, but the smoke still hung in the air.

Marc and I headed toward the taxi stand towing our exhausted children and two airport carts. We had eight pieces of luggage, but the black and yellow Ambassador taxis lined up at the stand were roomy. One Ambassador swallowed the four of us and all our luggage. It had no seatbelts, so Marc and I each grabbed a child and held him tightly.

My body ached after the 8-hour flight from Amsterdam. Our toddler had not slept at all. Thai Airlines had a designated Child Care Hostess on the flight; the official name tag worn by the lovely young attendant provided her title. She was concerned about John crawling on the carpets. "Strong cleaner on them," she said and picked John up off the floor. Then she made funny faces at him. I'm sure she meant well, but he screamed with alarm, so she deposited him back in my lap; then he wiggled his way back down to crawl in the aisle and was picked up again for funny faces and more screaming. Under his breath, Marc called her the Child Scare Hostess.

I wanted every one of us in bed asleep and quickly, but once outside the airport fence, our taxi stopped at the end of a long line of taxis at a gas station.

"They buy gas after they have a fare," Marc said.

In the three years that followed, I never saw an Indian worker waste a rupee. That same frugality was why our driver took off from the gas station into the black night—finally—with headlights off.

"Please put your headlights on," Marc said.

"Saving battery, *sahib*," the driver answered.

"Put. The. Headlights. On." Marc said.

The driver shrugged and pulled a knob on the dashboard. A cloud of weak yellow light landed on the asphalt six feet ahead of the car.

* * *

I would find my pleasures in India eventually, but at that moment, I was newly arrived, responsible for two little boys, and over-informed about health hazards. Before we left Philadelphia, my sons had shots for scary diseases like typhoid, yellow fever, and tuberculosis. I'd brought a year's supply of antimalarials for us. For diseases like dengue fever (called "bone-break fever" because that's what it feels like), I would have to trust to luck and the mosquito nets I'd brought for the boys' beds. To reliably ward off Hepatitis A, the boys would have needed a gamma globulin shot every 30 to 40 days, but a shot every month was a nonstarter, so, instead, my armaments would be boiled, filtered water and strict food hygiene. I didn't know if the kitchen at the hotel where we began our stay was clean, so, for the first few days, even meals at the 5-star Taj Palace felt like Russian roulette. My what-if self—easier for me to live with among the predictabilities of home—had come to India, too.

D1/35 Vasant Vihar

What became my home in India was tucked into a quiet neighborhood called Vasant Vihar. Wealthy Indian families and foreigners lived along its dirt roads. Our two-story, corner house was new, and the landlord, a ceiling fan merchant, and his family lived on the ground floor, which was partly underground. Their apartment opened onto the side street. On the main street, a wrought-iron gate eight feet tall blocked the entrance to our driveway; like all the other gates on the street, it was usually locked. Polished slabs of black and white stone supported the gate and joined a wall that surrounded the whole property. Shards of broken glass were embedded in the top of the wall, which gave me serious pause. The building itself was a hot-climate classic, whitewashed concrete-over-brick walls outside and inside with cool floors of white marble and pink composite stone.

Our home was a blank canvas when we showed up, and it stayed that way for a while. We'd brought little in our household shipment—clothes, disposable diapers for trips, toys, and a bed and highchair for John—and that shipment took three weeks to arrive after we did. It was cheaper for Marc's employer, the *Philadelphia Inquirer*, to buy us furniture in Delhi than to ship ours, so, within the first few days, we went to what was described by other expats as the upscale furniture shop in the city. We found ourselves in an incredibly hot second-floor showroom with open windows (and flies), where neon lights and ceiling fans (no air conditioning) clicked on and off as electricity dipped and surged. And the shop *was* upscale and sold beautiful teak furniture with simple lines, but I'd never literally dripped sweat buying furniture before. Making our way in intermittent darkness, Marc and I ordered a dining set, a couch, a bed for us, a bed for David, and a guest bed. Eventually, we filled in the house with cane-and-rope chairs, some side tables, and a bookcase, all bought from a cane merchant (*wallah*) who rode up to the gate uninvited with all his wares loaded on a bicycle.

Marc Kaufman

Cane Wallah and Wares

The cane *wallah* offered immediate delivery off his bike. But, like our household shipment, the store furniture took a while to arrive. So, our "home," at the beginning when we needed it most, was a set of empty rooms that echoed. Our home had nothing to do with the four of us; we just slept there on floor mats. As I bought Indian handcrafts over the years, it became my home, with primitive folk art and elegant miniature paintings on the walls; brass, copper, and earthenware jugs on the floors; and, on tabletops, small statues of holy men and nursing mothers made of Indian clay and baked by the Indian sun.

The biggest room had no specific function I could identify. Entered from the door to the outside hall, it sat in the middle of our living space like a traditional Indian courtyard would. Doors along its walls led to all the other rooms in the house. Eventually, I turned it into a kids' playroom for 100-degree days. I had a carpenter make a wooden playhouse and a small slide faced with some shiny laminate. I bought a few big baskets to hold toys. From a departing foreign family, I bought a kid-size red-enameled desk for John's art projects. Still there was a lot of open space. That room became our household's town square, where I consulted with the people who worked for us, viewed the spread-out wares of various itinerant merchants, and hosted John's playgroup. And it was a fitting place for the big, 1940s-style telephone that sporadically connected us to the rest of Delhi and the world. That big beast of a device was the only kind of phone available from Mahanagar Telephone Nigam Limited, the telephone utility whose unreliability drove even Indians nuts.

Opening into the center room were a living room, a dining room, a guest bedroom with bath, a kitchen, our bedroom with bath, Dave's bedroom with bath, and John's bedroom. Every room had a ceiling fan, and most rooms had big air conditioners mounted in holes cut through the walls. Those machines were like the window unit my folks bought in the 1950s only bigger, and they were LOUD. How loud? On a phone call, my sister-in-law asked, "Are you vacuuming while we're talking?" THAT LOUD!

Meltdown No. 1

Every day felt like a wall-to-wall challenge. Even an after-dinner walk with John in his stroller meant frequently hoisting him over broken sidewalks, big tree roots, and pig and cow poop. I was discouraged and exhausted, and the first of my India meltdowns came only several days into our stay. It happened at the American Community Support Association (ACSA) on Chandragupta Marg. A tiny building on the edge of the ACSA compound housed the American Women's Association (AWA) hiring exchange for household workers. Had I ever hired a servant before? Emphatically not. I was a plumber's daughter from a working-class town in New Jersey; my mother cleaned our apartment. At the exchange, I never got to the point of asking for workers' references. Instead, overwhelmed by how to hire a servant, the heat, and the lack of kid things I needed because of the delayed household shipment, I burst into tears. Heads turned, and, lucky for me, I caught the attention of a career foreign-service wife who was volunteering that day.

She walked over and smiled, introduced herself ("Joan"), patted my back, and determined that my most immediate need was a highchair for John, who'd been eating his messy toddler meals sitting on my lap. She took down our address and phone number and sent me deeper into the ACSA compound to the pool so the boys could cool off with a swim. By the time we got home, an ancient but sturdy wicker and wood highchair had arrived.

Later that evening, the phone rang. When I answered, the woman's voice on the other end sounded like all the people I'd grown up among near New *Yawk*. Each of her dropped -r's and added -w's grounded me in the reassuring familiar. I didn't know if my AWA volunteer chose the caller specifically for that reason, but Joan had lived abroad for years and might have known that the sound of a familiar accent soothes homesickness.

The caller introduced herself as "Harriet" and asked, "Can I do anything for you right now?" "Not right now," I said. "Well then, why don't you come by my house tomorrow for tea?"

Marc Kaufman

Harriet, the Accent from Home (right) and I

I did go for tea, and Harriet was exactly the kind of woman I liked—and especially needed then. She was a straight talker, funny and kind. Her son and daughter were grown, but she and her husband had been posted to Pakistan when their children were young. The children had survived nicely, and so would mine, Harriet insisted. Women like her went wherever they had to go and led family lives all over the world. They didn't embrace India in a showy way; they enjoyed what they enjoyed there, and they coped with and maybe bitched or joked about the rest. On hard days, when I felt like I was failing at my adventure, their company was easier than that of some NGO wives who preferred India to the States. I couldn't match that gung-ho attitude.

Harriet was clear eyed and casual about her challenges. After her umpteenth diagnosis of amoebic dysentery, she refused the icky Flagyl treatment that was standard for it. "Everybody's got to have a pet," she told me. "The amoebas are mine." And when I fretted about the many flights Marc and even the boys and I had to take, Harriet provided me with a different point of view. "An air crash is a quick way to go, better than hanging around in pain with cancer," she said. Her positive, quirky way of looking at things offered me a different way of seeing them. And her advice whenever I went into a tailspin about anything was always, "You have got to get past the fear." Sometimes I did …

And Sometimes I Didn't

My compassion lost out to my fear soon after we arrived. Building was underway on our roof for Marc's office and for a laundry room. As was common at construction sites in Delhi, the workers were an itinerant Rajasthani family. Everyone—from a white-haired grandfather to an infant who slept in a scarf hung in our bougainvilleas—came to work. Only the two small children didn't labor, the infant snoozing in the bougainvillea and a boy I thought was about 20 months old. In fact, I'd estimated his age with western eyes. As I watched him each day, I realized he was closer to four years old but small. He stayed in the hall out of the sun and played with a wooden top. Early on, I noticed that small patches of his skin were white and flaking, and after a while, that white crust thickened and spread. I had no idea what it was or if it was catching, and I became more and more nervous about my boys coming and going past him in the small hallway. I was new to the country and felt surrounded by threats I couldn't assess that demanded solutions I hadn't yet learned. A year farther on, I would have paid for a visit to a doctor and for medicine to treat the child; instead, I asked that he not come to work with them. The family wouldn't risk losing the job, so the boy stopped coming. I was left with shame for banning him and relief that he was no longer near my children. In time, India gave me many chances to explore my contradictions and my limits.

And I hit my limits so quickly compared to what an Indian, however poor, brought to his or her life. Like the blazing hot day when the grandfather among our builders burst into song on the roof. The monsoon failed that year, and Delhi was bone dry and over 100 degrees daily. But that day, for a short while, a light rain fell. On the scorching hot roof where he was building brick walls, the old man, dressed as always in a dirty white turban and loincloth, burst into song as the first drops fell. I couldn't understand the words, but I needed no translation; he sang his pure joy at the feel of the cool rain on his body. His full-throated thanksgiving continued until the shower ended. I grew in appreciation during my three years in India, but I never matched his grace.

Letter Home to an Old Friend
One Month In

July 15, 1987

Dear Diane,

Thanks for your letter. Two weeks on Cape Cod sound like nirvana to me now. India is an exotic, exciting place; it also is extremely difficult, even for the privileged few like ourselves. I'd consider our difficulties in getting settled rather funny (we've unpacked and repacked our suitcases eight times since June 23) if we weren't trying to solve them while caring for a bored, friendless 6 1/2-year-old who can't play outdoors (does 99 degrees sound too hot to you?) and a 16-month-old who just discovered tantrums and who broke out in chicken pox three days after arrival. (Can you imagine the opportunities for infections here? John lives on the floor.) Our most recent set of moves was occasioned by our electric meter board bursting spectacularly into flames one Friday morning—it happens to everyone at least once. And we have a <u>new</u> house. Many westerners here keep an electrician, carpenter, and plumber on retainer. Often there is no power in the neighborhood (kind of nice since then it's not my problem to solve), and city water runs for two hours each morning and two hours each night. People get sick a lot—vomiting, diarrhea, hepatitis, malaria, dysentery. This is in the capital city. How much traveling will I then do with the kids? How much of exotic India will I see? Marc is stationed here for three years, doing stories all over South and Southeast Asia—even possibly forays to Korea, China, Tibet ... I don't think the mistake is India; I think it's the combination of India with small kids. As for exotic, it's there, but too hot and dusty now to explore, so what I've seen is more borderline weird. People are building two rooms for us on our roof. Men build the walls, and women balance 10 bricks on their heads and climb the stairs to deliver them. A maybe-20-month-old baby of theirs sleeps on a burlap rag in my [hallway], rag shirt, no pants. One day I saw him eating chapattis [unleavened, whole-grain bread] and raw onion for lunch. Half-naked 4- or 5-year-olds beg *at the car windows at stoplights. Construction workers (whole families) live in tent villages at construction sites. Feral pigs and cows wander my (upper class) neighborhood. And everything that goes in our mouths must be sterilized. Maybe things will pick up.*

Write again.

Lynn

Daily Life

Marc's assignments took him into conflict zones in Sri Lanka, Afghanistan, Pakistan, and the Punjab. On one reporting trip to Afghanistan, he was fired on by both warring sides: shelled with the Mujahideen on the ground by Russian forces in the air then shot at by the Mujahideen as he flew over them in a Russian helicopter. If something happened to Marc, I would at least know he was doing what he loved. But at 4 a.m., awake in the dark and alone with my little boys, I couldn't picture what came after that for the surviving three of us.

His editor expected Marc to spend 70 per cent of his time on the road in South Asia. Watching our car disappear down the street with him inside was always a downer. It didn't matter if he was going as far as Haryana, the state next to Delhi, or to South Korea, my spirits sank at the start of his trips. Especially early on, before I made close friends with other women who had children, parenting solo weighed on me. I conjured up lots of what-ifs. Yet in retrospect, I think that parenting was also what kept me grounded. Permission for foreigners to do salaried work was hard to get from the Indian government, and Delhi could be a limited and lonely place for a partner with no responsibilities. But I had my sons and all that flowed from them as my job.

On weekdays, I got up with the boys and made David cereal or a peanut butter sandwich or toast with melted cheese. While Dave got dressed, I changed John and dressed myself. Once ready for the world, John and I walked Dave past the cows and pigs wandering through our neighborhood (and past quite a lot of their poop) to the school-bus stop and waited for the bus. I always lingered a moment or two after Dave climbed in to make sure the driver roared off only after Dave sat down.

Then John and I made a regular stop on our way home. Near our house at a quiet intersection, John climbed onto a low concrete platform where the two streets crossed. Standing as tall as he could and wearing a serious face, he directed what little traffic passed. Indian drivers smiled at John and obeyed his signals to stop or to go. On those mornings, I enjoyed how India and its people patiently indulged most children.

By the time we got home, Chote Lal, our cook, was in the kitchen making coffee for me and pouring milk or apple juice for John. Meera, the boys' *ayah*, arrived as we ate breakfast. Once she'd had a cup of tea, Meera asked for my "pro-GRAMME" for the day. If I was going out, she did a little craft project with John at home or took a walk to the playground with him. In cool season, they'd play ball on the roof, or John would ride his Hot Wheel in the driveway. If John was going out with me, she caught up on chores while we were gone. Sometimes, without me, she and our driver took John to the railway museum to ride its miniature train or to Lodhi Garden to climb on its ancient stone tombs.

Once a week, John and I went to a playgroup at friends' houses or hosted it at ours. When I joined the group shortly after it started, *ayahs* came with us to the get-togethers, but that meant children were outnumbered by adults. Not a good strategy for socializing kids to each other, so eventually we left our *ayahs* at home.

At midday, John and I ate lunch. Chote Lal frequently served bowls of instant ramen, which would not be my first choice. Each time, he'd beam at me and explain, "Johnny-ji wanting noodles, madame." John, as usual, had gotten to the kitchen before me and ordered *his* favorite lunch.

After lunch, John and I read books on his comfy floor mat, and he'd drift off to sleep for an hour or two. With the household on its two-hour lunch break and John asleep, I could do what I wanted. Early on I unpacked boxes from the move; later I wrote letters or read; sometimes I even curled up on the mat with John and snoozed.

After his nap, in cool season, John and I met Dave at the bus stop. In hot season, Jai Singh, our driver, took us on the 20-minute ride downtown to the American Embassy School (AES), where we'd pick Dave up, cross the street, and enter the ACSA compound to swim.

Back home again later, we'd have supper and the kids had baths. I read to John at night, consulted with Dave on his homework, and helped him memorize his "times tables." Before lights out, I read to Dave, too.

Once the staff left and both boys were asleep, I'd watch videos from ACSA—usually *Thirtysomething*—and eat fresh lychees or custard apples or (God help me!) Punjabi sweets loaded with *ghee* (clarified butter). Sometimes I'd have a 2-hour audiotape from my friend Carol to listen to in bed after my shower. She recorded them in her car as she drove from Philadelphia to Richmond to visit her family. In addition to all her news, I heard her friendly chats with toll takers along the way. And, always, before going to sleep, I read books about India.

On some days, I also chased down things we needed. With no big supermarkets or department stores and very little advertising, my shopping in Delhi was hit or miss. Someone must have pointed me to the Himachal Pradesh state emporium, for instance, where I bought the best apple juice in Delhi, John's favorite drink. I went regularly for a whole case because the juice, with lots of syrup added, was my only sure-fire method to get the bitter antimalarials into him. I went to Modern Bazaar for black-market western cereals. Sometimes I searched Khan Market for toys and hid them away for birthdays and Christmas. Barbie dolls had arrived in India, but what was available for boys—sturdy rubber balloons, wooden tops, cricket bats, kites, and ping-pong paddles that lost their rubber facing on first use—couldn't compete with American action figures. Through a friend, I found the clever carpenter who built the playroom slide and playhouse; those were big hits on two Christmas mornings. And Jai Singh regularly drove me across Delhi to get good coffee beans from South India and tea from the Nilgiri Mountains at a tiny shop that I found through another friend.

On some days, I went to meetings. I joined the parents' organization at school and volunteered on school committees. I joined the AWA and volunteered on its committees. I was team mom when Dave played in the soccer league at school. John and I went to all Dave's Little League games at ACSA, and, in the heat, we went to the ACSA pool so often that John's corn-silk hair turned green from chlorine. Visits to friends' houses and trips with the boys to places like *Appu Ghar,* an amusement park, or to the Delhi Zoo filled in some blank spaces.

In other words, I did all the mother-and-kids' stuff I did back home, which is how being a parent gave my daily life some familiar shape within the very unfamiliar context of Delhi.

Intimacy

Being a wife did not keep its familiar shape. Marc was often on the road; over three years, he repeatedly covered violent conflicts in India, Pakistan, Afghanistan, and Sri Lanka. For a clandestine run he made over the Khyber Pass to report on the Soviet-Afghan War, we set a date by which I'd hear from him. The date came and went, and I wondered how I could get back the body of someone who was not officially even in Afghanistan. His call came several days late; he was safe; I was relieved and angry. Violence wasn't the only threat. He was in Bangladesh during major floods, which disturbed the poisonous snakes that live there. Once he was lost in the Sundarbans, a mango forest and swamp of about 1,600 square miles in India and Bangladesh. His assignment was to write about the "tiger widows," women whose husbands had been killed by Bengal tigers while fishing or gathering honey in the Sundarbans. He went on assignments to Thailand, Burma, Tibet, and once for three weeks to South Korea. Even there, he covered protests that got violent. I understood Marc's love of adventure; it spoke of a curiosity that was attractive to me. But adrenaline and cortisol are friends when we need them for fight or flight and should ebb when the threat is gone. Triggered by situations I could only worry about, they stopped ebbing and became my body's background noise.

I was concerned for Marc's safety, but additionally, when he traveled, my responsibilities for the boys felt heavier without a partner. And when he called, the phone connections between us were often interrupted by electronic interference or by an Indian operator yelling *"Hanji? Hanji?"* ("Yes? Yes?") then hanging up. Those phone calls didn't leave me feeling connected to Marc. Sometimes I was so angry after a hard day, I didn't answer the phone. Take that! And when Marc was home, I wanted time alone, apart from my sons' needs and the staff's issues. Apart from everyone, in fact, including Marc. That was the opposite of intimacy.

Absence may make the heart grow fonder, but I've always depended on communication and trust between me and Marc. Lots of time apart under stress emptied the marital good-will account; we drew ours down to zero by the time we moved back home. So, intimacy was not without its challenges. But, unlike the previous two couples posted to India by the paper, we came home still married and remain so 35 years later. From my point of view, that covers the important facts about intimacy.

Our Household

Initially, our servants were the central people concern in my life. I made friends in India who were dear to me, but eventually my family there comprised the people who worked in our house. Like a family, we were together all day most days; like a family, we needed each other; like a family, we had to try—and sometimes failed—to understand each other. But unlike most families, we were shaped by different cultures that were not easily read by outsiders. And, hard for me, an only child who needed some time alone every day, there were so damn many people in my house.

Except when I slept at night, at least seven other adults were at home with me. Their work day ran from 8 in the morning until 8 at night, with a two-hour lunch break. Their work week ran six days, Monday through Saturday. If Marc was away on assignment, on Sundays I did solo shifts—cereal for breakfast, hanging out in front of the TV, a cab to ACSA, swimming at the pool, fast-food lunch at the snack bar, more swimming, dinner in the restaurant, a cab home, reading to the boys, and to bed.

I found that I needed a lot of helpers in the house in India. The cook shopped and bargained almost every day at the small markets he trusted, made sure our food and water wouldn't make us sick, and supervised the rest of the occasionally fractious household. The nanny took care of John and David when I was busy, did John's laundry, and babysat when I was out at night. Marc needed a translator and someone behind the wheel who could take him through complicated, sometimes dangerous situations, and the driver did both. When he wasn't away with Marc, he drove me and the boys safely through the scrum of Delhi traffic. We had no washer or dryer, so the laundryman hand washed and ironed our clothes twice a week. And the maid, who worked six half days each week, swept all the floors and cleaned them with disinfectant every day; she also did the rest of the housecleaning and helped the cook when needed. A daytime or a nighttime guard always sat by the gate— living, breathing burglar alarms. I wasn't convinced we needed the protection, but the gate was kept locked, so we at least needed someone to open it. On Marc's work visa, we were India's guests, and India needed jobs for its people. At our peak, we employed nine Indians, some part time and some full time. Eventually, I stopped looking over my shoulder for a grande dame when one of them walked up to me and said, "Madame ... ?"

If having all that household help sounds cushy, in part it was, but it didn't feel like an unmixed luxury. The servants did what was hard to do for ourselves (no supermarkets! no vacuum! no washing machine! no babysitting teenagers!) or what we didn't need to do in the States (boil and filter all the water! sterilize raw fruits! run back and forth to a locked front gate!). I miss the people who worked for us, but I don't miss all that help in my house. I don't envy wealthy people with big households. The interruptions, questions, complaints, and requests of my large staff percolated constantly, and to ignore them was to leave my home without a CEO.

Lynn Litterine
Ram, Margaret, Chote Lal, Jai Singh, and Meera, with David and John

A web of obligations and benefits bound us together. Our cook ran the household and decided who got anything we weren't going to keep. Marc and I settled issues that went beyond the cook's authority. We approved raises in pay. If someone was drunk at work, we set the conditions for continued employment. Drunk again? It was up to us to fire him. We provided all of them with cash for small bridge loans and paid for visits to doctors and for medicine. We paid for school uniforms for some of their children. On an American salary, we could afford to do all that; the hard part was to figure out what Indian pay and benefit norms were. On arrival, I knew nothing about going-rate salaries, but as I met other foreign families, I learned what they paid. More importantly, as I got to know the people who worked for us—and the people who worked for other foreigners—I learned who in my house was invaluable. And, on the theory that there was no perfect objective amount, we paid a little more than the foreigners I'd polled. I hoped that strategy would make the staff feel valued and would earn us their loyalty. I never regretted that decision; they took really good care of us.

All that said, let's meet the fine people who, like my Indian handcrafts on our walls and tables, eventually made that empty house a home. They were the Indians I was with most, and they were the Indians I came to know best.

Chote Lal, Our Cook

Marc Kaufman

Before we left for India, Marc showed me a photo of Chote Lal, his first and most important hire. All I could say was, "He's very skinny for a cook." But Chote Lal, slender and soft spoken, was the Steady Eddie of my household for three years. He was honest. He was pleasant. He was kind to my boys. He was hardworking and took justified pride in his cooking and in keeping us healthy. Okay, his sweet-and-sour mutton meatballs were barely touched by us, but only Marc ever liked mutton no matter how it was cooked. And Chote Lal's water-buffalo lasagna—perfected when he cooked for Italian diplomats—tasted as good as any lasagna I'd ever had. Most impressively, he kept us healthy at home in a country where hepatitis, amoebiasis, and bacterial dysentery were endemic. To kill germs, he soaked our fruit and vegetables in "pinky" (a solution of potassium permanganate in water that turned neon pink) and rinsed them in water that had been boiled and run through a ceramic filter. In fact, he boiled and filtered all our cooking and drinking water and even the bath water for John for as long as John was apt to put bath toys in his mouth.

I think we were a relief for Chote Lal. Years of living overseas can loosen some folks' inhibitions, but we were Steady Eddies just like him. He told me a story about foreigners he'd worked for. I can tell only what Chote Lal described; I can't speculate on what it meant. A party was planned by those employers, and, among preparations for it, Chote Lal was asked to buy the head of a water buffalo at the market. Water buffalo have huge heads and thick horns that can be quite long. A recipe for a water buffalo head was not in Chote Lal's repertoire, but he was only asked to leave the head somewhere in the house out of the way. Then he went about cooking for the party. That night, when he helped carry trays of food up to the roof where the party was, the entertainment had already begun. This is what he saw: "Madame, one man is in his underpants only, and he is wearing the water buffalo head over his head and dancing crazy all around." Chote Lal told me that, then shrugged and gave me a noncommittal smile. To happen upon that scene unexpectedly must have been a shock for Chote Lal, but he, Marc, and I were a smooth fit. Two of the three of us shouted occasionally or slammed a door, but Chote Lal was dependably well behaved. He set the standard for decorum in our household, and he set it high.

From the time we met, he saw his job as easing our way through each day as comfortably and pleasantly as possible, which brings to mind his homemade banana bread. Initially, we moved from the hotel to the *Washington Post* house until our house was ready. The *Post* family was on home leave. The first time we moved from the *Post* house into our own, Chote Lal greeted us with a loaf of warm banana bread and the gift of a tiny brass figure of a Brahmin priest. As various devices in our house—fans, air conditioners, the electric meter board, the water pump—broke down over the two weeks that followed, we moved back and forth between the *Post* house and our own. Each time we arrived back home, Chote Lal had yet another fresh loaf of banana bread ready for us. The machine breakdowns were not his responsibility, but he felt it was his responsibility to welcome us home and to cheer us up again. In difficult times, a lot may be said for homemade banana bread, even without walnuts.

We were barely settled in at home when I almost lost Chote Lal, which freaked me out because I knew early on how much I needed him. On the afternoon when the upset happened, Marc was away on assignment. Before he left, he gave Chote Lal the big, wooden shipping container that our household things had finally arrived in. Maybe Chote Lal planned to use the container himself, or maybe he planned to sell it; all that wood was a good "get."

The staff was on midday break; our second grader was at school; our toddler was napping, and I was enjoying the quiet down time. Suddenly someone was banging on the door. When I opened it, Chote Lal stood outside crying and talking fast. At first, I understood only the words "I quit," and my heart sunk. "Why?" I asked.

He explained between shaky breaths that our landlord had confronted him, demanded the shipping container for himself, and threatened "to cut off my head, Madame, if I don't give it." I was new to India, but I already understood that power was sometimes brutally exercised. Our landlord, Mr. Bhartia, was wealthy, and wealth translated into power. But the background issue that also terrified Chote Lal was sectarian. Our landlord was a Sikh, and although Bhartia was short, chubby, and out of shape, Chote Lal knew that some Sikh men carry a dagger or sword as part of their religious regalia. That gave the beheading threat some oomph, and recent events in India shot it sky-high for our Hindu cook.

There was a bloody history to his fright. That history was so recent, in fact, that the real estate agent asked Marc if he'd prefer a different rental when he showed him the house. "*Siddharji* (Sikh) houses were targets in the riots," the agent said. "If you don't want this one, I'll show you someplace else." In 1984, three years before we arrived in India, Prime Minister Indira Gandhi, a Hindu like Chote Lal, had ordered Indian troops to take back the Golden Temple, the holiest site of Sikhism. Radical Sikhs occupied the temple complex in Amritsar and were agitating for greater autonomy for the Punjab, the state where Sikhism was founded. The battle that followed Gandhi's order killed about 1,000 civilians and soldiers, and many of the dead were Sikhs. Some months later, two of Gandhi's Sikh bodyguards shot her dead in her garden in Delhi. In the riots that followed her murder, Sikhs across India were killed; most of the deaths were in Delhi.

Alone on a quiet afternoon in hot season, I found it hard to assess Bhartia's threat, but two thoughts took over: first, I must not lose Chote Lal, and second, the landlord would not cut off my head. We had already handed him an athletic bag full of cash to cover our first year's rent. With two more years expected, we were worth more to him than an empty, wooden shipping container. I also assumed that none of that first cash installment had been reported to tax officials. If I needed a threat of my own, I had one.

I left Chote Lal composing himself in his kitchen, went to the Bhartias' door, and banged on it. A servant answered. I tried for a dignified, authoritative tone with more than just a hint of anger. "Bring Mr. Bhartia to the door now, please." My nerves calmed a little when my landlord appeared. He was shorter than me, and, in his brown polyester leisure suit, he looked more like a large meatball than an assassin.

"This container is my husband's," I said, waving my hand dramatically toward it at the end of our driveway. "My husband has given it to our cook. It now belongs to our cook."

Bhartia paused and then gave the little sideways shake of the head that in India means, "I disagree with you, but you have the upper hand here, so we'll do it your way." All he said was, "As per your choice." Chote Lal kept the container and his head and I kept my cook.

* * *

Chote Lal was the one who had presented Ram as a candidate for daytime guard, and he probably earned a fee from Ram for doing that. But his recurring moneymaker with the guard was something else. He had a trick that Ram always bet against; Ram never thought about the last time it was performed, when, as always, he had bet against Chote Lal and, as always, lost money.

The performances occurred whenever Chote Lal had a coconut in the kitchen to use in a curry. He bet Ram that he could whack the coconut open with his bare hand, and Ram would take the bait. Chote Lal set three dry beans in a triangle on the marble floor of the kitchen and balanced the coconut on the beans. He raised his arm overhead, paused for a moment, and brought his hand down in a karate chop to the shell. Wham! The coconut always split open, spilling its milk across the floor, and Ram always had to pay up.

Lynn Litterine

Chote Lal Breaking Yet Another Coconut Open Bare Handed

I once asked Chote Lal when Ram wasn't around how he did it.

"Thinking through to the other side, madame," he said.

Ancient wisdom and I left it at that.

* * *

My younger son is now a veterinary surgeon with a gentle approach to his patients and their owners. Although we usually had pets and cared for them well while he was growing up, I attribute John's compassion to Chote Lal. One instance: kindness to ants.

Our home in New Delhi was brand new but not well sealed. While cool season was never cold enough for the drafts from under doors to matter, the gaps did matter during dust storms, when red grit blew in, and after John's meals. The many bits of food that fell to the floor from his high chair signaled silently to ants who lived beyond the dining room doors. The ants entered the room under the closed doors to the garden in a workmanlike single file. In the household hierarchy set by Chote Lal, what John left on his plate was Margaret's, our maid, to eat, but the food that dropped on the floor was the ants'. They took 10 minutes tops to carry the bounty outside in the same orderly line they had entered in. Occasionally, however, the ants got too ambitious and went exploring in Chote Lal's kitchen. That was forbidden. He wouldn't harm them but instead confronted the ants with a broom made of long, soft grass, with which he gently ushered them out the kitchen door to the Bhartias' courtyard a floor below.

"Ents [sic] coming in, Madame," he would tell me if I happened into the kitchen then.

His approach to insect control became so ingrained in John that, circa age three, he scolded me when an almost-three-inch water bug spooked me and I stomped it. We had just emerged from a shower in the locker room at ACSA when the bug skittered past and I crushed it. John was furious.

"He didn't do anything to you," John said, emphasizing each syllable in outrage.

I had to agree. I could be cruel when frightened, and John held me accountable for that unthinking cruelty. My insect-killing policy now is limited to squishing mosquitoes that are in the act of biting me and to drowning in the toilet ticks I pull off family members and pets. Other insects I let be or usher out the door as gently as I think Chote Lal would.

Meera, Our Ayah

The boys' nanny taught me gentleness by example, too. When we hired her, Meera was 19 years old. She was a pretty young woman with a lilting voice and a sweet willingness to do any work Chote Lal or I asked of her. And unlike my working hands, which went at things like they were killing cats, Meera's hands were slow and gentle. They seemed to caress whatever task she was doing. That was appropriate when she massaged the boys' scalps with oil, a chore she insisted on doing regularly; then, her hands clearly communicated affection and patience to my children. But even hand-washing John's stinky diapers, I never saw her rush what she was doing. Her hands seemed to move to the luxuriously vast rhythms of Indian time; nonetheless, she accomplished a lot with them—washing all John's laundry, making all the beds, helping Chote Lal when needed, putting everyone's clean clothes away, always being available when John needed her. When I start to rush through a chore now, I picture Meera's hands and how they gave respect to any work she was doing. Then, I try to slow down and give all my work the time and attention I owe it.

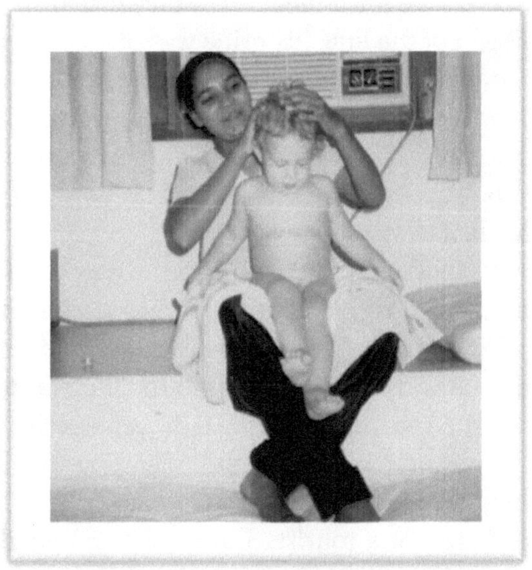

Lynn Litterine

Meera and John Scalp Massage

Meera understood that David, who was five years older than John, would ask for her help when he needed it, and she would also let others in the household help him. But with John, she was territorial, except with me. I learned that early on. Since we had no washing machine, our clothes were laundered during two weekly visits by Nanda, the *dhobi,* and put back in the dressers by Meera when done. Dirty laundry was all the same to me, so I assumed all of it would be washed by Nanda, including John's clothes. But as I pulled the diaper pail out into the center room and piled John's dirty clothes next to it for Nanda's first visit, Meera came over to me.

"Excuse me, Madame, please," she said, managing to sound both firm and respectful. "I will wash Johnny-ji's clothes and diapers. I am his *ayah*; that work is mine."

And in the guest bathroom, for the three years that followed, she did all his wash. She sang in Hindi as she pounded John's clothes on the marble floor of the shower. Even in hot season, in spite of the steam and the smell of pee and sweat that filled the room, she sang on and never hurried.

As traditional as she could sometimes be, Meera somehow understood American wisecracking. She got that I liked to laugh and make others laugh and that I meant no harm by it. For instance, when Chote Lal brought his daughters, he lined them up as they exited an auto-rickshaw. Standing at the head of the line, his pride was obvious. They were lovely young women dressed in *salwar kameez* (tunics and pants), one in lavender, one in yellow, and one in pink. Indian women skillfully mixed the colors of their clothes, but many Indian men wore monochromatic outfits in dull colors, and on that day, Chote Lal sported a dark gray shirt and matching pants. I leaned in toward Meera and whispered, "He looks like *koa* (crow) surrounded by *totas* (parrots)." Meera clamped her hand over her mouth to trap the laughter, but her eyes danced. We both respected Chote Lal immensely, and we both enjoyed mischief, too.

When Meera was with me, she became my bargaining agent in the markets. If a price cited was too high, she'd draw herself to her full height, about five-foot-four, and stare down the offending merchant. "Do you think I am a foreigner? Do you think I am a tourist?" she'd ask. "I am not a foreigner, and I am not a tourist, and my Madame will not pay that price." "My madame"! I loved belonging to her, never more than on the first Hindu holiday she organized for us.

Marc was away, and I was feeling blue, but that evening, Meera came back after her shift ended. She wore a deep blue *saree* of what looked like heavy silk—not her workaday cotton *salwar kameez*—and she carried a big bag out of which came everything she needed for a *Diwali* observance: incense sticks in holders; candles shaped like Lakshmi, the goddess of prosperity, and Ganesha, the god who removes obstacles; little animal statues made of sugar or of clay; tiny clay oil lamps (*diwas*, hence *Diwali)* with hand-twisted cotton wicks; a marigold *mala* to encircle the Lakshmi candles; a coconut with sacred red thread tied around it; fruit; and Indian sweets topped with silver leaf.

The rest of the household hung around after work to see the ceremony and share the food, and the boys enjoyed the ritual and the sweets. It wasn't one of *my* traditional holidays, but it was a holiday, and it wrapped itself around me. We were a household gathered to voice our hopes for a good year to come, and I settled into the feeling that I belonged. My mood was much lighter when I finally headed off to bed several hours later.

Lynn Litterine

Meera, Dressed Up for Diwali, with David and John

Meera fit easily into our family and quickly became "MeeMee" to all of us. She did more than put up with our American ways; she enjoyed them. She was traditional but also had an independent streak I respected that brought her trouble sometimes. She was the topic of gossip both in the nearby village where she lived with her family and among the older, married ayahs of my friends. She respected Chote Lal like a father, but her best friend in the household was our driver, Jai Singh. That made sense; he was as bright and as fluent in English as she was. And both Meera and Jai Singh were young people who'd grown up in Delhi, an urban center. But of greater significance to the Indian community, he was a man and she was an unmarried young woman. Their friendship eventually became a problem for them and us.

Jai Singh, Our Driver

Delhi's streets and highways are crammed with bicycles, scooters, auto-rickshaws, cars, buses, trucks, and bullock carts. Families of as many as five, all without helmets, zip past on the utilitarian black bicycles of India's lower-middle class or on the aqua-blue scooters of the middle-middle class. Cows wander slowly through the chaos. Horns are preferred over brakes as all those vehicles weave in and out around each other. Indians drive on the left side of the road, not my comfort zone, and, although I worried incessantly about germs, the only foreign child whose death I heard about in three years in Delhi died in a traffic accident. Any risk from an accident was upped back then by mobs that quickly surrounded mishaps. They made a rapid judgment on fault and, especially if someone had been hurt, used stones from along the roadside to punish whomever they thought responsible. Driving in India was a blood sport, and I never got behind the wheel.

Jai Singh drove our "Ford Falcon color yellow," as it was described in the newspaper ad where Marc discovered it. The car was from Australia, used, and Marc chose it because it enveloped our family in a cocoon of high-quality steel. But the engine was as cranky as the body was strong, and getting foreign parts was difficult to impossible in India's closed economy.

Any breakdown meant a search for cannibalized parts at roadside garages. I say "garages" but most were tarpaulins stretched between bushes for shade. Underneath, jumbled piles of used parts covered the ground, and a couple of skinny men squatted among them. But those men were masters of the ad hoc and could get a car running again with a smile and a paper clip; they were fazed by nothing. Searching for parts among the "garages" was tedious, and we were limited to taxis while our car sat unused, so breakdowns were annoying. We realized we had been too free in venting our annoyance when we heard 3-year-old John call our car the "for fuckin' color yellow." We toned down our language after that.

I would have preferred the iconic Indian car, a Hindustan Ambassador. The Ambassador's roomy design is the same as the British Morris Oxford Series III. In fact, the British Motor Corporation sold both the manufacturing rights and the tooling for the Series III to Hindustan

Motors in 1956. The Hindustan Ambassadors first rolled out in 1957, and the company produced those big beauties until 2014. Ambassadors have a silhouette like my dad's '49 Chevy, and, like that Chevy, the interior feels like a room on wheels. Ambassadors are heavy cars with small engines, so a fast 0-60 is not in their skill set. In fact, I never saw one get within sniffing distance of 60.

Marc drove our "Ford Falcon color yellow" in Delhi when he had to but preferred to have Jai Singh at the wheel. And I got into the driver's seat once in three years. The entire household came out to watch as I backed down the driveway at a stately pace. I can't remember why I had to move the car, but I can remember how strange it felt to drive again.

Jai Singh was a crucial member of the household for Marc. On assignments to dangerous and remote parts of India, his driving skills protected the two of them in snow on winding mountain roads and through threatening mobs. Also crucial was his ability to read what was going on in the culture around them. And since his English was fluent, he was Marc's interpreter.

He was important to me as well, just as important as Chote Lal and Meera, because without him, I would have had to bushwhack Delhi on my own in a taxi or be stranded at home. When Marc didn't need the car, John, Jai Singh, and I explored Delhi. After breakfast on those days, John went out into the driveway and, still diction challenged, called out "Dai Ding." A chipper "Coming, Johnny-ji" issued from the staff quarters, where the men in our household hung out when they weren't working. Jai Singh came down the stairs double time, I strapped John into his car seat (eventually I'd found used seatbelts), and the three of us set off for places I'd read about in my guidebooks.

At first, we went to well-known sites: Humayan's Tomb, a huge building that looks like a gingerbread palace and is topped by a Mughal dome; the nearby *Purana Qila*, a fort from 1538 that housed Japanese internees during World War 2 and then Muslims heading back to Pakistan during Partition; *Jantar Mantar*, an astronomical observatory built in 1725 but with the playful look of a Disneyland ride; *Qutub Minar*, the city's tallest minaret; and *Hauz Khas*, a neighborhood peppered with Muslim tombs and fashionable shops. Although the tombs in *Hauz Khas* were centuries old, children were welcome. John scrambled all over them and was never scolded by an attendant; in fact, smiles followed him. The sight of my toddler in loud surfing shorts climbing over ancient Indian architecture was absurd and delightful to me, too.

After a while, I'd seen Delhi's best-known sights, so we branched out into its religious life--Hindu temples, Muslim mosques, and Sikh gurdwaras. I was welcome anywhere in the temples and gurdwaras. And even in the Jama Masjid, one of India's largest mosques, I was allowed in the huge courtyard of the complex. As an unbeliever, I was forbidden entry only to a Zoroastrian fire temple.

The big Hindu temples were crowded and loud, an interesting but overwhelming riot of color and motion and sound and smell. As Jai Singh understood what suited me better, we went to smaller temples that weren't as easily found. Once we took John to a temple on the Yamuna River dedicated to Hanuman, a monkey-faced god who was a favorite of our driver. The only sounds in that peaceful, hidden-away place were the chattering of its resident macaques and the rippling of the river shallows. We'd brought bananas for the monkeys who lived there, and John was excited.

"The monkeys can bite, Madame, so I will hand them the fruits," Jai Singh said. Then he scooped up John with one arm to watch the action at monkey level. The solemn-faced macaques grabbed and gobbled one banana after another as John laughed and bounced on Jai Singh's arm.

Our explorations broadened as my reading about Delhi broadened. Soon I was finding out-of-the-way places like an austere temple of the Arya Samaj, a reformist Hindu sect, and a cemetery for Christian missionaries, where bird song softened the tombstones' testimony to epidemics and early deaths. Not all our destinations were religious. We found a district for fine handmade furniture where I watched as a rosewood table I'd ordered was inlaid with brass and mother of pearl. And at a market where men carved traditional Rajasthani chairs with woven rope seats, I asked a workman to fix the Ganesha on one chair because it was missing its belly button.

Delhi was packed with interesting places to discover and explore, and John and I had a plan whenever the car was ours. I was pleased when Jai Singh, born and raised in Delhi, told me: "Madame, with you I have seen places in Delhi I did not know existed."

Ram, Our Daytime Chowkidar

I met Ram, our daytime *chowkidar* (guard), the day we arrived at D1/35. He was standing at the foot of the driveway and delivered a smart salute as our car rolled in. The strangeness of being saluted on arrival at my own home was made stranger still by what Ram was wearing. An olive-green bath towel was knotted around his waist; the short sarong (*lungi*) was hot season attire for rural men. I didn't know how long Ram had been in Delhi, but his wardrobe was still "village side."

Chote Lal had recruited Ram as our house guard because, he said, Ram was "strong." I could see why Chote Lal thought so; Ram wasn't muscular, but he was chubby compared to our slender cook. Almost immediately, Ram asked Marc for a gun, which seemed unnecessary because we lived in a walled compound, where the surrounding streets were the responsibility of the Delhi police, who were armed with automatic rifles. Marc said no to the gun but yes to a *lathi*, a long, stout stick. Happily, Ram never had to use even his *lathi* to protect us from marauders. His dozing presence in a wicker chair by the gate apparently kept criminals at bay for three years. Our night chowkidar was a quiet young man who spent his whole shift studying. I knew him only by his silhouette in Ram's chair near the gate, and he never had to deal with any burglars or thugs either.

As the only one who lived full time in the quarters behind the house, Ram's most crucial chore was to listen for the moment when water came through the municipal pipes in hot season. The daily schedule for that was approximate. At the sound of a trickle, Ram ran to our water pump and turned it on. For however long the water sloshed through the pipes ("ran" doesn't describe the scant flow), he pumped it to a tank on the roof that would get us through the next day. You could order a tanker truck of water, but we never did that. Skipping showers and following "Yellow mellow, brown down," we got through. Although once, when the temperature was 100, and no water ran in the Delhi pipes for 16 hours, I moved the boys, Meera, and myself into a 5-star hotel. Top-of-the-line hotels always had water. Not only did it flow abundantly from the taps in the bathroom but also into the hotel's swimming pool, which was kept full. India could be challenging, but money could always buy some ease.

Ram was with us for most of our time in India, but when we came home one night and found him drunk in his own vomit on his driveway chair, Marc issued a warning: a repeat would mean the loss of his job. When it happened a second time, Marc fired him. Ram didn't seem to hold a grudge, though; he smiled and waved whenever I ran into him at a nearby market.

* * *

That was our full-time staff, the people whom the boys and I lived with six days a week, twelve hours a day. We also had part-time staff, who worked for us anywhere from six half days a week to a half-hour weekly stop-by.

Margaret, Our Inside Sweep

Marc Kaufman

Margaret and Meera Dressed Up for Christmas

Margaret was an ethnic Indian and a Christian, whose family was among the 300,000 Indians driven out of Burma in the 1960s. She cleaned our home and often helped Chote Lal with holiday meals or when we had guests for dinner. Her main responsibility was to clean the stone floors with disinfectant every day because 15-month-old John spent a lot of time on the floor, and we continued the practice for three years because older kids slept on floor mats and played on the floor and watched TV from the floor and dropped snacks on the floor and then picked them up again and ate them. Margaret scrubbed the floors with grace. No grunt-punctuated kneeling on the stone for her. Instead, she stood upright and moved a wet rag across the floor with one bare foot, her toe rings glinting under the ceiling lights. Every day, she did all the floors with that one bare foot. It must have been the cleanest, strongest foot in Delhi.

Chote Lal parceled out to the rest of our household what we didn't use up each day ("garbage" in the States), and Margaret got to eat what John left on his plate, which was often a lot. She got chubbier while working for us, and I was pleased because I knew she had troubles. One day she came to work with a black eye; her husband had hit her. In the States, I would have known what to do, but in India, I couldn't assume I did. I wouldn't call the police. The police were hard on anyone who wasn't wealthy; Margaret and her husband might be asked for *baksheesh* and be roughed up if they couldn't produce the bribe. I also didn't know if she'd be safe at home with her husband if I took any action. And even if Margaret was willing to go to one, there were no women's shelters. So, I hugged her and asked if we could do anything for her. She wept and said no and thanked me. To my relief, she never came to work with a black eye again.

Margaret was also at the center of a mystery Marc and I never solved. A man no one in the household knew left a neatly handwritten letter for us one day. It read:

Respected Sir or Madam,

> I am very sorry to write this letter because I wanted to inform you some very important matter. But I don't want to tell my name.
>
> Your servant (Mrs. Margaret) is taking all your (doller) [sic] money. She is telling me the child [sic] through out but I am keeping back. No sir she took your doller nearly 35 thousand. If you want to check keep your doller the same place in counting. After she go to the house if you follow her you can find so much doller in their house.
>
> Before coming to your place she is working in Moti Bagh. She rough [sic] one ring (gold) but they gave complaint in the police.
>
> So, Sir or Madam, please check her you will get all your money in Madras she brought [sic] new house about 35, 40 thousand. Where she is getting all these money? From your house all doller.
>
> Please don't tell her you got letter. Just you follow her and catch her. Her husband is in No. 60 Poorvi Marg. That man also doing the same business.

So Sir, save your money.
Thanking you.

Sir, and Madam,
    You please go and check in Vasant Marg. If you check you will definitely find.

It was a ridiculous accusation. Even if the 35,000 referred to rupees, not "dollers," it would have been $2,000, and we never had that much cash in the house. And what cash we had was in a locked closet; like a good Indian housewife, I kept that closet key and the one to our storeroom on a chain that always hung from my waist. Margaret couldn't have found anything more than spare change around our house. Those facts were obvious to us, but it was also a fact that someone had written that letter, whatever it was designed to accomplish. In Delhi, telling tales on other people, true or not, could be a method of community control, an expression of jealousy, an attempt at revenge, or even a shot at a coveted job. We'd never know what the writer's purpose was, but for due diligence, Marc called Margaret to his office and told her in private what the letter said. That brought Margaret to tears. Marc also told her that he didn't believe the letter—and he didn't—but Margaret was now aware of the accusation and of an accuser. We hoped that would be enough to put an end to whatever was going on, and it did.

Nanda, Our Dhobi

Marc had two little brick-and-mortar rooms built on our roof. One was his office; it held the Associated Press wire machine and was where he worked when he was at home. The other was a laundry room for Nanda. *Dhobis* (laundrymen and -women) pounding clothes on rocks along Indian rivers are a classic scene, but Nanda was a sophisticated New Delhi laundryman. He was used to working for foreign diplomats and businessmen whose household shipments included washers. Our shipment had not, and he washed our clothes by hand. Nanda accepted the job on one condition: "Please do not tell other foreigners that I am doing your washing by hand." I think the issue for Nanda was convenience, and I honored his request. He did great work, and no one outside our household ever learned that he did it by hand.

Roshni, Our Outside Sweep

Castes who clean inside a house do not clean outside a house, and castes who clean outside a house do not even enter the house. I was a guest in India and tried not to tread on peoples' sensibilities, whether they matched my own or not. Roshni swept our driveway and outside steps. She worked crouched down in a squat and wielded a yard-long broom made of slender branches. I had no idea why the driveway or steps needed sweeping, but we added Roshni to the payroll for twice weekly visits, and she never missed a workday. She was quiet, efficient, and thorough. I know she must have stood up when I paid her or as she came and left through the gate, but I can't remember how tall she was. I remember her only in that crouch moving crablike as she swept the ground.

Our Gardener

We had a small garden between the front of our house and the wall surrounding the whole compound. The garden held a wooden swing set

I'd bought from a departing foreign family, some potted plants, and a lawn of what the *mali* (gardener) called Mexico grass. The grass was grayish green, and it grew in fuzzy bumps that looked like small animals and were springy underfoot.

The *mali* would show up regularly but on no schedule I could figure out. I never learned his name. He spoke no English, so my only dealings with him involved my forcefully repeating "No *khad*! No *khad*!" whenever I saw him in the yard. *Khad* (fertilizer from human feces) was still in use then, even in city gardens, and I didn't want it around the kids. "No *khad*, madame, no *khad*," he'd repeat after me in the only conversations we ever had.

On his visits, the *mali* would stand silently watering the garden from a dribbling hose. Watering took a long time because pressure was low to nonexistent. The garden work, like all work, was done in the Indian way; human hands and hours of workers' time substitute for infrastructure. If you had a lawn and money to spend, you paid someone to stand for as long as it took to wet down the grass. Watering the grass was the *mali*'s priority, but he also grew pretty flowers in our "winter garden" from December to early March.

* * *

With all that household help, I had no pressing chores, tiresome errands, or yard work to do, and that was pleasant. But our home was crowded with more people than I was used to, and those people were my responsibility in ways that were unfamiliar to me. They were not just employees and they were not quite family members; they were a hybrid of the two. We spent 60 hours a week with the full-time staff; we liked them as people; we employed them as workers; we depended on them for our wellbeing. Our relationship was a challenge I hadn't faced in my middle-class American life, and it was a challenge whose full context I never completely understood. The imbalance of power between us and them was too great, so they would understandably answer any questions in the way they thought we wanted them to answer. Early on, Marc and I spent hours when we were alone trying to decode various staff members' behavior, but eventually familiarity and acceptance replaced our attempts to understand everything. In that way, too, we were like family members

The issues I didn't foresee arose so suddenly, they gave me no time to think—Chote Lal and our landlord fighting over a shipping crate or the letter we received about Margaret stealing money or the time I caught sight of the men bringing prostitutes into the servants' quarters. Or even Dave's first birthday party in India, when Marc was away on assignment, and my exuberant household overwhelmed the family celebration. The men were as rowdy as the kids, only bigger and tipsy. Dave loved all the jumping around and yelling, but we seemed to be on the edge of adult chaos, and the guests were as unreadable to me as our party norms were to them. I had lost control of my home. Then, Chote Lal, of course, with impeccable timing, brought the cake out, and the roughhousing stopped. We gathered around the table, and Chote Lal lit the candles. Dave made a wish and blew them out to a round of applause, and John and I sang "Happy Birthday."

Lynn Litterine

As Obstreperous As the Kids Were, Only Bigger and Tipsy
John, David, Jai Singh, and Ram

Each person in our household had a gift for Dave. In the face of such kindness, I felt embarrassed about my worries. But I had no way of knowing where the hijinks would end, and not knowing was always the hardest thing.

And Then There Were Our Landlord and Landlady ...

Mr. Bhartia was introduced to me through his fight with Chote Lal. His idea of who had the right to that shipping container differed from ours. His wife, Parminder, differed from my sense of what constituted social preliminaries.

When Marc introduced me, she fingered the bangles on my wrist and opened with, "Why are you wearing silver instead of gold? You're rich."

"I like silver," I said.

Her follow-up question to that was, "Did you have a love marriage?"

"Yes."

I had no sense of how to continue the conversation, so it ended.

My understanding of rented space diverged from hers, too. Her house was new, and she was proud of it. Having shown friends and relatives her apartment downstairs, she would arrive with them unannounced at our door to show them through our rooms. I made clear that the visits were not welcome, so she conducted tours of our garden instead. I'd catch a glimpse of her colorful *salwar kameez* as she and a few other ladies walked around outside and peered in through the window panes of the dining room doors. When Meera tried to fend off those tours, Mrs. Bhartia told her, "You're too protective of those foreigners."

The Bhartias meant us no harm. Two couples simply arrived in the same house from different planets. Each of us behaved as we'd been taught was acceptable. I think it's possible that the Bhartias and Marc and I never understood a single thing the other couple did. Some culture gaps are too wide, and I believe that it was a gap in culture, not in character or kindness. We never knew each other well enough to weigh those qualities.

Bhartia norms remained mysterious to the end. In the last year of our stay, our landlady cornered Marc outside and asked if he ever went to Singapore for work. When he said he did, she asked if he'd bring back a refrigerator for her on his flight. She'd pay for it, of course, she told him. Marc declined.

Marc Kaufman

The Bhartias

The Supporting Cast

I needed even more suitable people than our household staff provided. I needed a pediatrician who was comfortable with a questioning American mother. I needed a banker who saw nothing strange in my showing up for a cash withdrawal with an athletic bag for the money. I needed the *wallahs* who arrived at the house with goods that I had no idea where to buy in Delhi. I needed the *sadhus* at my gate who asked for alms and promised good karma because who doesn't need good *karma* on an adventure. I even needed the beggars at my car windows so I could model both compassion and common sense for my sons in a place of overwhelming poverty. And although I didn't need the police, they showed up anyway to check on us.

Dr. Taneja, Our Pediatrician

In the late 1980s, doctors in India were not accustomed to being questioned by patients. Their norm was don't-worry-dear-I'm-in-charge. But I was an American mom, and my relationship with the boys' pediatrician stateside had been based on the doctor answering my questions. In fact, I kept lists of non-urgent questions between checkups. The first pediatrician I visited in Delhi was a woman who assumed that only she asked the questions. We were not a good match. Then someone pointed me toward Dr. Arvind Taneja. Indians have a charming gesture of respect, usually for elders, in which they touch a person's shoe and then their own foreheads. Although we were close in age, I would have happily touched Dr. Taneja's shoe. Born, raised, educated, and trained in India, he knew all about conditions there, but he had also trained for a while in the States and was comfortable with a pushy mom.

But he asked me the first question, and it was a riveting one: "They've had their rabies shots, right?"

And I did not have the right answer.

No. *No! No! No!*

I asked their American pediatrician about rabies shots, and he said rabies vaccine was only needed by people who worked in labs with live viruses. The boys wouldn't need it in India, he said. I don't remember the percentage of Delhi street dogs that Dr. Taneja said died of rabies, but it was high enough to cause me distress. Those feral dogs were near the heights of my animal-loving kids, and they were all over Delhi streets. I felt hysterical, but Dr. Taneja weighed in with the first of many doses of calm. "Don't worry. I can get you French diploid vaccine for them," he said. "Bring them back next week."

I had no idea what "French diploid vaccine" was and I didn't care; if it was good enough for Dr. Taneja, it was good enough for me. I wanted it shot into my sons' arms yesterday, and Dr. Taneja, as promised, delivered it in a week.

He also gave my boys their Hepatitis B shots, but it took Marc's parents to get that vaccine to us. Again viewed from back home, it didn't seem that a second grader and a toddler would need the shots. Hep B spread through needles or sexual contact. But we were already in Delhi when a friend's husband, who was a pediatrician for CARE, told me that anecdotal evidence indicated the disease might be transmitted in other ways as well. So, when Marc's parents visited us in December 1987, they carried Hep B vaccine in a cooler from New York to Delhi, including a tourist stopover in Bangkok along the way. They also carried a pogo stick that Dave had asked Santa for. Stellar grandparents those two!

Most visits to Dr. Taneja came about because of John's breathing. He didn't have asthma before we moved to India, but once there, it became more of a problem with each cold he caught. Dr. Taneja estimated that a third of patient visits to his office were for asthma. He attributed it to air pollution, and that was long before *The Guardian* newspaper reported on a 2019 *Lancet* study:

> "Pollution accounted for nearly 1.7m premature deaths in India in 2019, or 18% of all deaths, according to a study that lays bare the human cost of the country's toxic urban air."

Dr. Taneja put John on a "puffer" that I had to use at the first sign of a drippy nose.

"It's a good medicine," he said. "The plant's been used for breathing problems since ancient Egypt." He was right about the medicine working well, and he was right on another thing, too. "When you're back in the States, John's asthma will gradually disappear because the air is cleaner." We'd been back home two years when I realized I didn't know where John's puffer was anymore.

Our Bankers

Paying a year's rent with an athletic bag full of cash required understanding local bankers. I don't know how other banks handled their money, but I suspect that, like our bank, they had a clear sense of both the need for cash to pay big tabs, like a year's rent, and for the need of discretion regarding the Indian tax authorities. We were led to our bank by the *Inquirer* correspondent who preceded us. Because business in India was personal, my transactions at the bank always included a cup of tea at the desk of our banker. He was a fat man who never stood up. Instead, as we sipped our tea, his assistant, a predictably thin man, ran all the required comings and goings. My host guided the thin man with hand signals, and the assistant knew the choreography so well that no words were exchanged between them. I would give them a check for U.S. dollars in the amount of the rupees I needed. Dollars were prized all over South Asia, and I was asked not to fill in a payee's name. In exchange for that blank line, a 10-per-cent cash bonus was added to my rupees. That must have been illegal, and it's why I'm not using the names of the fat man, the thin man, or the bank. But that blank payee line never backfired on us, and I hadn't come to India to change how Indians did business in their own country.

Eventually I learned that the boss took to his feet occasionally. During the winter holidays of *Diwali* and Christmas, he and his assistant came to our door with season's greetings and a bottle of good Scotch. But, like Santa, they had a long list of stops at customers' homes and didn't accept my invitation to come in; they just got back into their car and took off into the night.

Wallahs

A *wallah* is a man (at least the ones I met were all men) who sells a specific item (cane *wallah*) or does specific work (train ticket *wallah*) or is being identified by where he lives (Delhi *wallah*). We had gate-side visits by *bandar wallahs*, whose trained monkeys made the boys laugh, and by *kobara wallahs*, whose cobras, winding slowly up out of their baskets at the sound of the *wallah*'s gourd pipe, fascinated the boys into uncustomary silence. But most *wallahs* who came to our gate sold things:

Kashmiri lacquerware, brassware from Uttar Pradesh, rugs from Kashmir, handmade-lace garments and table linens from South India, wooden boxes inlaid with designs in camel bone from Rajasthan. And like our cane *wallah*, they all traveled with their wares on India's familiar black bicycles.

Because *wallahs* brought handmade things from all over India, an hour's visit with any one of them was entertaining. But my favorite *wallah* sold a black-market commodity—wine from overseas. I had access to his wares only because he trusted Chote Lal. As the seat of government, New Delhi had many diplomats, and they entertained a lot. They were entitled to quarterly duty-free shipments from abroad. Bottles of wine left over from their last allotments showed up on the black market, sold by the diplomats themselves or given to or pilfered by household staff who sold them on. Some of those bottles eventually reached our wine *wallah*.

He showed up at the gate on his black bike unannounced and according to no set schedule, an almost-bald, oldish man, missing a few teeth and wearing a soiled white *kurta pajama*. I was always happy to see him because some fun lay ahead for me. He carried into the house two big, brown-paper bags with celery stalks and carrot greens sticking out of the tops. Once inside, he pulled out the vegetables and set them aside; they were just camouflage. Out of one bag came bottles of white wine; out of the other bag came bottles of red wine. The wines were from all over the world. France. Russia. Italy. Argentina. Germany. California. He charged one price for reds and a slightly lower price for whites. "People liking red more," he said. The reds could be delicious, expensive French wines or Russian wines that tasted like cough syrup, same price. The whites were as wildly varied. I didn't know anything about wine, but I could afford to experiment for prices that hovered around $8 a bottle. We drank some beauties and we drank some stinkers. I have never had so much fun buying alcohol.

Sadhus

Infrequently, a *sadhu* (mendicant holy man) would ring the gate bell. I had to let go of the need for certainty in India, so I decided to assume they were real *sadhus. Sadhus* are ascetics who live on society's fringes and seek *moksha* (release from the cycle of birth, death, and rebirth) by self-denial and contemplation. Our *sadhus* wore saffron robes or white *lungis* loincloths. They had symbols, usually Siva's trident, drawn on their foreheads in white, yellow, or red powder, and their moustaches and beards were uncut. Their hair was also uncut and hung in long dreadlocks or was wound into a topknot bun the size of a cantaloupe. By giving them a few rupees, respectfully delivered at the gate by Meera, I earned good *karma*. That seemed like a great deal. I always needed more good *karma*.

Policemen

In 1987, Indian policemen on the streets were armed with automatic rifles. That was the first time I'd ever seen such a gun out and about on a street where I lived. Those guns are so big, I was taken aback at first, but eventually I stopped noticing them. By then, I'd even gotten used to the regular visits Delhi policemen made to my gate. They usually arrived two at a time and asked Meera, who'd answered the bell, "Do the foreigners still live here?" She'd say "yes," and they'd leave. They never asked for *baksheesh*, and I never gave them any. They seemed to be checking on us, but I never understood why. For three years, I tried never to draw their attention more than that, and, for three years, I succeeded.

Beggars

Riding the streets of Delhi meant dealing with beggars, who waited at most traffic lights to approach cars. They gestured at our car windows by moving their hands to their mouths as if eating or by holding out cupped hands for rupees. Nasal, pleading noises and grimaces accompanied the gestures. Beggars who were lepers would come up to the car and exhibit the stumps of their fingers or point to the flat place where their nose should have been. With my two little kids watching, I needed a policy on giving. India's need was great, and we could not fill it. I wanted the kids to learn a compassion that was also sensible.

So, first, my policy had to be affordable. I couldn't give money to all the beggars who came to the car windows, so I ignored the able-bodied ones who could work. The policy also could not make a bad situation worse. Some beggars had disabled limbs, and I'd heard about gangs who maimed poor people and ran them in begging operations. Some gangs sent child beggars out, and I wasn't going to hand cold cash over to the local Fagins either. Money would only encourage exploitation, so I gave to both those big and little people things like oranges and firewood and matches, all of which were expensive, useful, and, I hoped, of less interest to the men who ran the gangs. For lepers, my policy had to be grounded in a greater kindness. I gave rupees, a little over 16 cents' worth to each, the going rate expected from foreigners. Although drugs were available to treat leprosy, many uneducated Indians viewed the disease as *karma* inflicted for misdeeds in past lives, and that karmic view produced a passivity in seeking treatment: "It's my fate, madame." The cruelty of that view was as criminal as the gangs, and I felt that the bit of cash we handed over had to come with a smile and without shrinking away from maimed hands and faces. Those were the responses I wanted the boys to see.

Letter Home to an Old Friend
Four Months In

October 4, 1987

Dear Diane,

I'll say this for being in India: I'll never be able to feel sorry for myself with quite the conviction I used to have. I'm amazed to see how poor a person can be and still not just lie right down and die—still smile, in fact. Astounding. David started school Aug. 10, second grade at the American Embassy School—1/3 American, 2/3 from other countries. He likes it well enough …. He's lost patience with India right now. He was being a good sport all this time, but now he's sick of the heat, the food, the dirt. I hope he'll even out over time—it's hard to make my own kid unhappy for the purpose of our adventure. … We went to Srinigar last week … After dry, dirty, dull Delhi, Kashmir was heaven—cold, rainy, moody, its people with craggy mountain faces and some with bright blue eyes, that sense of magic at being in the bare beginning of the Himalaya … I think the Delhi heat (low 90s to 100 now) is starting to sicken me—I'm nauseous all the time here, like early pregnancy … But it's interesting to be here, frequently awful, but interesting. I'm just stale—the hot weather traps me indoors with my toddler more effectively than a February snow storm does at home … Best, Lynn

Trying to Understand

If We Could See Ourselves as Others See Us

At my first Back-to-School Night in New Delhi, the principal shared a story that he heard from a longtime missionary to India. The audience of parents at AES came mostly from the States, Europe, and East Asia. And some newcomers, including me, felt like they'd left earth and landed on the moon. The principal, an American himself, knew that we needed a shift in perspective.

"This missionary was in a village preaching to the villagers," he began. "He was encouraged and pleased by their attention and stopped for a moment to let a point sink in. As he paused, he took out his handkerchief, blew his nose, and returned the cloth to his pocket. When he continued the sermon, he was distressed to see that no one was paying attention anymore. He kept speaking but was clearly no longer connecting with the audience. He was mystified as to how he'd lost them. Finally, one man in the audience dared to raise his hand.

"'Yes?' the missionary said.

"'Excuse me, sir, may I ask you a question?'

"'Certainly,' the missionary answered.

"'Sir, why are you keeping that?' "

Given the gift of that story, I never again judged an Indian for blowing his or her nose straight onto the ground. Saving snot in a pocket *is* an odd practice that warrants a hard look.

Culture Defines Time

I was unprepared for the Indian approach to time, too. I had always lived in a temperate climate, never a hot one, and I took seriously the hourly, half-hourly, quarter-hourly, and minute marks on clocks: TV shows on the hour, medical appointments on the half hour, news updates every 15 minutes, and "wait a minute, sweetie" when my kids wanted something right away. But Indian time was elastic. When to arrive when invitations read "dinner at 8," but dinner began at 10 or 11? Clearly not "on time" as I understood the concept. But eventually, even for me, the heat produced a slow-motion feeling that stretched passing hours. Time just felt different.

Time in India was different in another significant way. The people I lived among and tried to understand consulted sacred texts from the 3rd century BCE that describe time cycles so vast, I could not imagine them. Hindus set the length of a *kalpa* at 4,320,000,000 human years and define it as 12 hours in the life of Brahma the Creator. The length of the larger *maha-kalpa* is 311,040,000,000,000 human years, which makes up Brahma's full lifespan of 100 years. But wait, there's more! In the Causal Ocean, where material reality is created, Brahmas beyond counting rise and burst like bubbles in repeating cycles forever. Time does not advance in a line forever as it did in my western mind.

Fitting into an Indian sense of time—and the heat—slowed me down. Eventually, I showed up at 8 o'clock dinner parties around 10; eventually, I didn't wriggle impatiently on store lines or in offices when clerks took tea breaks; eventually, I sat back and enjoyed a restaurant meal that proceeded at snail's pace. Eventually those huge cycles of Indian time framed the west's Newest New Things differently for me; all the bright, shiny stuff, latest events, people in the news, and ground-breaking ideas that I found so interesting back home became underwhelming. They came; they went; eventually no one remembered them. No one object, person, feeling, or thought mattered over much in that Indian time scale. What I lost in self-importance, I gained in perspective.

A Sense of Self in the Cosmic Ocean

Within those vast cycles of time, a self seems insignificant, but a self is still needed to navigate one's life. What I saw Indians use to ground themselves was their inherited communities. What class and caste was the person born into? What state was a family's father from? What village was he from? What does the family cook and eat and what is forbidden to them as food and drink? What work are they allowed to do? What work is forbidden to them? What clothing do they traditionally wear? What gods and goddesses protect them?

When Meera talked about those markers, she didn't chafe at them; her voice instead reflected pleasure in the order they created, whether she described the cooking spices people use, the clothes they wear, or how she could read their religion and sect by looking at them. Her society was not a self-fashioning one, and she seemed to accept that. She was a Hindu and a *vaishya*, a class of farmers, traders, and merchants, and she had been born into a sub-caste of metal workers near Moradabad. *Karma* from her past lives dictated the family she'd been born into. Within that family, she was a daughter, younger sister, and aunt in a net of relationships with prescribed rules and clear and certain consequences for breaking them. She was subordinate to men, even her young nephew to some extent, and to older women. To me, her life seemed hemmed in by other people and rules, but she loved her family and talked happily about each person in it and the rules that determined their behavior.

The inherited past seemed fully present in most Indian lives. I met many skilled craftsmen, and I always asked how they'd learned their craft. Their answers were always the same eloquent wave of a right hand back over a left shoulder that meant "from the people who came before me." They sought excellence in technique, but they did not seek innovation. Close adherence to tradition was the priority.

But tradition can be cruel and backward when it sets social contexts. As with the untreated lepers who begged at intersections, belief in *karma* encourages damaging passivity because it anchors lives in an unyielding past. Understood as the effect of actions in past lives on current fate, it draws an obscuring veil over individual and societal agency in human misfortune. "It's my bad luck," I often heard Indian people say when something went wrong. The causes of that "bad luck" were hidden in other lifetimes and were not explained by individual mistakes or social injustice that could be corrected in this one.

Still, Indians carry their inherited selves as naturally as they breathe. They don't default to an Important Separate Self as I did because Hinduism discourages that. Instead, it insists that a separate self is an illusion that evaporates when examined closely, a disappearance that marks both a return to Oneness and liberation from the cycle of birth, death, and rebirth.

"Get over your small self," India advised me.

So Many, Many Selves

In 1987, 819.7 million people lived in India. That number brings to mind news photos of packed trains on the morning commute into Mumbai or of teeming masses crossing Kolkata's Howrah Bridge. I was never in that crush of Indian humanity. My sense of the press of people came instead from never being alone. Never. People worked in my home six days a week. Our staff seemed uncomfortable when the boys and I were alone at the dinner table. At least one person usually stood nearby and awkwardly entered the conversation now and then. Dave, who was taught not to interrupt, was outraged. "How come THEY get to interrupt, and I don't," he'd hiss at me. I tried to explain, but he was only 6.

Our full-time staff worked 12 hours a day, but even after they left the house at the end of those long days and my boys were asleep, I wasn't alone. From a window, I saw our night *chowkidar* in the wicker chair at the gate. And apparently one *chowkidar* wasn't enough even in our quiet neighborhood. When I read in bed or woke up to pee, I heard the neighborhood *chowkidar* thump his *lathi* stick on the ground as he made his rounds of the surrounding streets. I had no idea who hired him or who paid him; we were never asked to contribute anything. But awake at any time of the night, I knew that within minutes I would hear his thump as he passed the house. In India, someone was always nearby. Life in that crowded matrix rubbed me raw sometimes, especially when I was trying to sleep.

Sleep has always been an escape I could count on. With enough of it, I feel ready to meet the day's challenges. Without enough, I feel shaky. Marc was often out of town, and then the boys and the household were my responsibilities alone, and I needed to be rested and ready to go in the morning. When Marc rented the top half of the Bhartias' house, our landlord promised that he would stop running his fan business from the downstairs apartment. That promise was even in the rental agreement. Nonetheless, in the courtyard right underneath my bedroom window, little delivery trucks gunned their engines day and night. And at around 11 p.m., when the trucks had left, Mr. Bhartia's household enjoyed a noisy dinner in that courtyard. Each time we complained, Bhartia said it would stop. And then it didn't. It's difficult to make someone do something differently when they keep agreeing to do it as you've asked but don't. Indians were expert in that strategy: a sideways waggle of the head and a soberly stated "as per your choice," problem solved! Except sometimes it wasn't. That triggered my second meltdown.

One night, the trucks had been rattling through the courtyard for several hours. Drivers chatted loudly and flung boxes of fans around.

When that traffic ended, the household sat down to a lively supper with loud radio music. My id took over. I started bellowing while still in our apartment. I flew out the door in robe and slippers and pounded on the Bhartias' door. A servant opened the door, and I demanded Bhartia.

"Sahib is at dinner," Ganesh said.

"I know he's at dinner! I can hear him! Get him for me now!"

After a few minutes, Bhartia appeared. I stated my demand: "Everyone out of the courtyard! Now! I cannot sleep!" I'm sure he hadn't a clue why I asked him to quiet things down; 11 was a normal enough dinner hour for Delhi. He promised to do it anyway, "as per your choice," and we retreated to our own apartments. But even Screaming Crazy Foreign Lady in Robe and Slippers was not wild enough to get things changed; soon the trucks and noisy dinners went on below my bedroom window again. Solutions to some people problems in India seemed not to exist, a hard concept for an American to take in, but I finally developed a coping strategy. In hot season, in monsoon season, and even in cool season, I ran my big bedroom air conditioner full tilt for white noise all night every night.

Tragedies Erupt

During my first anxious months in India, both a son of Jai Singh and a son of Ram died suddenly. Two seemingly healthy, well-loved little boys—like my little boys—gone with no preamble was inconceivable to me.

One morning Jai Singh, who lived in Delhi, was late to work. When he called, Meera answered the phone, was silent for a moment, then wailed, "Jai Singh's son is no more." I don't know how Ram received his sad news from his rural village; he sometimes hung out at a nearby market, so a market phone may have been his emergency contact. Jai Singh's son was an infant in a middle-class family. Ram's son was a young boy back in his father's village. Each was healthy, developed a fever, and quickly died. I'd heard the developed world's cliche that life was cheap in Asia, but those fathers and the other people in our household held life dear, especially the lives of children. What was different between me and them was the expectations we brought to life. In India, the death of a child was tragic but not extraordinary; back home, it was extraordinary.

Jai Singh told me he thought his son might have been born too soon after his toddler older brother and might have been weak because of that.

He blamed himself for that timing. Ram just sadly announced his loss to me and asked for time off. Back with his family at their village, he would perform a Hindu ritual that would be turned upside down as the father did funeral rites for the son. When I asked Meera what caused each boy's death, she said, "Fever, madame. Fever." Explanations ended there. No tests or autopsies were done, none of the urgent searching for a reason like in the States, only Jai Singh's puzzling over his possible role in his son's death. Ram seemed to quietly accept his loss. A basic fact of life in India was that children died of sudden fevers. My household subsided into sadness for a while, and the people sought solace where they could, possibly with the gods.

Gods Are Just Like People ... Only More Powerful

Indian gods have full-blown personalities; they're like people you know. To understand India at all, I had to learn about them. I couldn't gauge how literal Indians' belief in them was—did Brahma, Vishnu, and Siva actually exist somewhere? But that question wasn't the important one for me. I wanted to know what qualities the gods represented to Hindus. The productive question for me was, "What do you see when you look at [insert deity's name here]?"

Bala Krishna (Child Krishna) is a pudgy, butter-stealing toddler and the object of loving indulgence by his devotees. In a country that frequently stared starvation or lethal fevers in the face, a chubby toddler god made sense. Pudgy cheeks and dimpled arms and legs were armor against hunger and illness, and they seemed to be the goal of all Indian parents who could afford them. Wealthier kids were chubbier; poorer kids were skinnier; really poor kids had distended stomachs and hair like rusty straw. For context, consider these statistics: In 1990, the childhood death rate in India was 134 children per 1,000 (Statista); In the United States that year, the rate was 9.2 (CDC).

Bala Krishna is not just a chubby boy but a spirited, naughty boy as well. Nonetheless, like my sons, he draws approving smiles from Indian adults for his rambunctious behavior because they know children are treasures that can be easily snatched away. Feistiness stands a child in good stead; a spirited child might be more likely to survive. "Oh, he is too naughty," Meera purred over John. "Thank heaven," I thought.

While Meera cooed over Bala Kirshna and John, when she spoke about Krishna as a young man, her affect changed; she became a *gopi*, the cow-herding girls whose devotion to Krishna is unconditional. When Krishna the Heart Stealer plays his flute, the *gopis* leave fathers and husbands at home and dance in the moonlight with the dark blue god. Hindus are careful to say that Krishna provides a holy ecstasy and steals "only saintly hearts" (https://vedantasociety.net/blog/krishna-the-stealer). But when telling me about him, Meera sounded like a teenager with a crush: "Madame, he is sooo handsome." Like many young Hindu women, Meera didn't date, and her community kept a close eye on her behavior. Some day she would enter an arranged marriage. Meanwhile, Krishna was a handsome love object, and her devotion to him would never get her into trouble at home or in her neighborhood.

Jai Singh was devoted to Hanuman. The monkey-faced god's loyalty to Ram, the hero of the epic *Ramayana*, spoke to our driver. In the epic, Hanuman literally moves a mountain to help Ram. "He reminds me that I must always do my duty," Jai Singh said when I asked what the god meant to him. That reassured me because, while the boys and I stayed in Delhi, Jai Singh accompanied Marc on some hair-raising assignments.

Ganesha, the elephant-headed god, is the remover of obstacles, a power symbolized by his elephantine strength. In some stories, his strength is also shown by his mastery of the rat, shrew, or mouse that accompanies him. In those stories, the rodent represents the ego, a suspect element in most Asian religions that is also out of step with Indian community values.

Ganesha also rules over beginnings, so I hung his statue next to our front door. Maybe, as we came and went, he'd advance whatever we were up to; at the very least, his good cheer, pot belly, and enthusiasm for candy made us smile. A fat, jolly god with the strength of an elephant was a good companion. And a little less ego on everybody's part kept the household running more smoothly.

Female gods are as ferocious as Ganesha is jolly; they battle the demons of the Hindu universe. In Assam, at a temple in Guwahati, a priest gestured toward a statue of his goddess and told Marc, "This goddess fierce. This goddess non-veg." She sounded like the relative to avoid at family gatherings. But to her devotees, as non-veg as she is, she is the ideal of maternal strength. Goddesses are mothers who would step in front of a car to save their child, and the car would lose.

Lynn Litterine

Ganesha

Durga is one such. A goddess of war, she rides a tiger or lion and carries a weapon in each of her many arms. Kali wears a necklace of skulls and severed limbs. She is violent but only when necessary, and her violence is righteous. Even Siva, the god of destruction, treads carefully around her. I had a special fondness for Lakshmi, the goddess of good fortune. John and I wound up in some rough straits during his birth, and a neonatologist named Lakshmi brought life back into his limp, gray body. She gave us the good fortune of John. So, on Diwali each year, the boys and I drew

Lakshmi's footprints near the front door to lead her into our home for good fortune in the year to come.

Hindu gods and goddesses engaged me. Nothing was simple with them, and that fit my sense of life on earth. In India, I had to think about both the multiplicity of gods and goddesses and the foundational Unity underlying them. India asked me to hold many dualities in my thinking. In a universe of never-ending cycles, destruction is the essential companion of creation, not its opposite; neither is possible without the other. Male and female also are not simply opposites. The goddess paired with any god is his *shakti*, the active energy of his power, and the two of them are fully potent only when entwined. Opposites are fully implicated in each other. My western world of opposites strictly separated by backslashes—creation/destruction, male/female, gentle/fierce—began to seem arbitrary and artificial to me. It also seemed much less interesting.

Visiting the Gods' Homes

In temples where the gods are worshipped, I saw rituals that were new to me, and, silhouetted against them, I saw better who I was. I felt at home in quiet places, like the little Hanuman temple where John and Jai Singh fed bananas to the macaques. I liked the visual calm of Arya Samaj temples and Sikh *gurdwaras*, where literal depictions of gods are not allowed.

The Hindu Kali temple in Kalkaji in Delhi is neither quiet nor calm. My visit there was my first to a big Hindu temple. The site was packed with devotees, and a din rose from hundreds of people praying. For me, the noise, the crowd, and the temple's vividly painted statues elbowed quiet thoughts away. The experience overloaded my senses, and I felt smothered, not spiritual. The big temple to Bala Hanuman (Child Hanuman) near Connaught Place was marginally less crowded but presented a challenge I hadn't faced at Kalkaji. *Prasad*, food blessed by first being offered to the main idol, was handed out to visitors at the entryway. I didn't want to offend by refusing it, but flies crawled on the food, and I knew the other things flies crawled on in Delhi. Meera armed me with a gracious way to turn down food from a god. I lowered my eyes and murmured, "It's my time." A menstruating woman is not an acceptable recipient of *prasad*.

Closer to my own sense of the spiritual was that Arya Samaj temple I visited. Although I'd grown up among the statues of the Roman Catholic Church, in my adulthood their literalness put me off. Deep reality seemed beyond depiction; the simpler, the better for me, and the Arya Samaj, a 19th-century reformist branch of Hinduism, rejects "stone idols." From the outside, the temple was an unassuming concrete building that was hard for even Jai Singh to find. Inside, a blackened fire pit occupied the center of a big room on the walls of which Vedic verses were incised in Sanskrit. The sacred fire and the chanting of Vedic verses constitutes Arya Samaj worship. Elemental fire and the reading of a text were abstract and bookish enough for my tastes.

Sikhs also organize worship around a text, and they consider that text, the *Guru Granth Sahib*, a literal guru. Books feel like living things to me, too. While I read them, my mind is in conversation with them as if with a person; the best books have their own affects that I can recall later like I do with people I meet; and I am a slightly different person after interacting with a meaningful book as also happens with some people.

Our family traveled north to Amritsar to visit Sikhism's most sacred site, the Golden Temple. A pedestrian causeway runs out into a man-made lake where the sanctum sits. That structure is sheathed in copper plates covered with gold foil. The *Guru Granth Sahib* rests on a platform in the sanctum 20 hours a day, and worship centers on one page opened at random each morning near dawn and chanted. The temple was another bibliocentric worship site where my mind could walk through the door that words always open for me.

Sikh *gurdwaras* are open to all, but parts of mosques are open to women only under certain conditions. Once I went to explore the *Jama Masjid*, a huge, historic mosque in Old Delhi, but was told that the prayer hall and minarets were only open to women accompanied by a male relative. I so wanted to see Delhi from the minarets that I tried to pass Jai Singh off as a male family member, but his jet-black hair and brown skin and my red hair and white skin sabotaged the effort. I'm glad now that they did; it would have been wrong of me to be so disrespectful. I did tour the courtyard, and I can say that a courtyard that holds 25,000 worshippers at a time is an impressive courtyard indeed.

I did slightly better at the *Jama Masjid* than I did at a Parsi fire temple. At the front gate of the Parsi temple, a sign prohibited entry to non-Zoroastrians. By 2019 the prohibition still stood, as I learned in an online article from the *Indian Express*. A suit was filed by a Hindu man named Sanjjiiv Kkumaar, who claimed that the fire temple was "practising a system of apartheid, untouchability and communalism by not allowing Hindus, Muslims, Sikhs, etc. to enter the sanctum sanctorum ...." The temple addressed his suit in a response:

> "The present petition strikes at the very foundation of the Zoroastrian faith professed by Parsis .... Barring entry to non-Zoroastrians in Zoroastrian places of worship is not based on factors like caste, colour or race nor is it discriminatory ...It is only meant to uphold and maintain the rules and laws that govern the protection and integrity of the sacred fires and the pledge taken by the first band of refugees from ancient Persia not to adopt conversion in India." (indianexpress.com)

I couldn't find reports of a case settlement, so I probably still can't visit the temple.

What I Liked a Lot and What I Didn't Like at All

I knew before I left the States what some of my challenges would be in India. The microbe menu would be broad and deep. The heat would be beyond anything I'd ever experienced. I would parent the boys alone a lot (check boredom, worry, and fatigue), which meant I'd allow them more on-screen time (check guilt). Other potholes in the road just sprung up in front of me after I was there. I also found unexpected delights in Delhi. Those delights were India's alone to offer me, and they were the aspects of day-to-day India that made me smile, laugh, and feel the specific pleasures of being there. Delights and complaints both have to be placed on the scale of my India.

Complaint: Health Issues

I discovered that my most challenging health problem was my own imagination because usually I did not imagine good things ahead. I saw threats to the boys' health everywhere, some of them even based in reality. Delhi's plethora of germs included bacterial and amoebic dysentery, giardia, hepatitis, cholera, rabies, dengue fever, Japanese encephalitis, and malaria. I went to elegant dinner parties where flies, ignored by guests, crawled on outdoor buffets. Dave picked up on my concern and once reported to me that Margaret had filled an ice cube tray from the tap. I emptied the tray and told Margaret to always—*always*—fill it from the ceramic-filter tank that held boiled water.   Kudos, Leftenant Dave! Signed: Commander Mom

But the boys and I needed to enjoy life in India, and we needed friends, so out we went into the larger world, which was not under my control. Occasionally, we paid for that with gut problems. I began saving empty film cans for ferrying stool samples to the doctor. Marc took the photographs for his articles, so my supply of cans was steady. I ran samples to our neighborhood pathologist, Dr. Singh, whenever the kids' GI tracts acted up. Dave's first all-night bout of dysentery was during our first year. John's first bout was that year, too. Dysentery causes explosive, watery poops, sometimes with blood in them, and that was alarming. Chote Lal never failed me with his hygiene, but we all ate at other peoples' homes and had no idea what went on in their kitchens. At the house of one of my friends, the cook felt overworked but said nothing. Instead, to cut back on his workload, he stopped boiling and filtering the drinking water. Dysentery promptly ran through the whole family.

Once I found Dr. Taneja, the boys' illnesses became less scary. On Mondays through Fridays at least, I could go on to someone I trusted. After a while, I became friends with the wife of an embassy doctor. I could visit her husband at home on Saturdays and Sundays when Dr. Taneja's office was closed and John developed one of his wilting fevers.

Although I found good Indian doctors in Delhi, big Indian hospitals were places to avoid back then. Wealthy Indians and foreigners went to private, freestanding clinics run by specialists, often married couples. While the wife delivered babies in one part of the building, the husband did neurosurgery in another. Although the clinic buildings looked like big private homes, the medicine performed in them was excellent. The boys would have been fine at a private clinic; nonetheless, I felt lucky that for three years my sons confined themselves to cuts I could close with butterfly bandages from my first aid kit.

Being in an unfamiliar country whose threats I couldn't foresee produced a steady buzz of concern. A visiting western chemist told me not to feed the boys cauliflower, John's favorite vegetable. "The pesticides on it here are carcinogenic," he said, "and it's impossible to scrub them out of all the little crevices." A nasty home-invasion robbery at the house of a friend of Dave's, a home Dave sometimes visited for overnights, rattled me. When three armed men forced their way in, his friend's father feigned a heart attack to scare them off. The ploy worked, but it doubled the terror of his wife and two sons, who didn't know he was faking. Another friend's children romped with some cute puppies at a playmate's house. A few days later, the dogs tested positive for rabies, and my friend had to schedule shots for her three kids. I could have focused on everyone's survival in the home invasion or the fact that rabies tests were done on the puppies in time, my friend was alerted, and her children got the needed shots. Instead, I got stuck on how I could ward off all the dangers, an impossible goal that led only to anxiety.

Delight: Cross-Cultural Fender Benders

The absurdities that unfolded when people from very different cultures collided made for funny anecdotes. Those "aha" moments, like the missionary's saved snot, made clear the extent to which each of us is submerged in our own familiar culture. Our customs are arbitrary and look bizarre from beyond our own cultural horizon. The silliness of some of that not only provided laughs but also put "shoulds" in perspective.

Simpler "aha" moments often involved language. The Indian term "cousin-brother" took me a while, but I finally understood it as either a relative outside the nuclear family but as dear to the speaker as a brother would be or as a person unrelated by blood but still as dear as a brother to the speaker. No one ever used "cousin-sister" with me; I'd need a sociology or anthropology degree to explain why.

Chote Lal's "same same different" mystified me until I realized that it meant exactly what he said: mostly the same but somewhat different. For example, "Chote Lal, is this the cheese you bought before?" "Same same different, Madame." Translation: "It's a different brand but the same kind of cheese and tastes pretty much the same."

Our cook's offer of "nice cafe" puzzled me at first because the cup of coffee that followed that offer was swill. Some rooting around in the kitchen cabinets turned up a jar of Nescafe. Chote Lal drank tea and had no way of knowing how awful instant coffee tastes.

I made Meera laugh the first time I asked in Hindi for tea with sugar and milk. "*Chai chini doodh,* please," I said. The sequence sounded ridiculous to her. She explained that "milk" (*doodh*) had to come first. "*Chai doodh chini,* madame." I figured it was a "peanut butter and jelly" kind of thing.

A misunderstanding Marc had with Ram did *not* make Ram laugh. Marc asked him to get rid of the "crows" nesting in the tree by our gate because they flew aggressively at anyone who passed by. Our Hindu *chowkidar*'s eyes widened in terror. "I no kill cows! I no kill cows!" he said.

At one point, I forbid Marc to make any more cleaning requests of Margaret after he asked her to clean the fabric edging of a Buddhist scroll he'd bought. Margaret's aim was to please, and her thorough cleaning of the whole piece smeared the painting. When Marc discovered that, he thought he should advise her in greater detail on the ways she might clean things with a lighter hand. "No, no, no. I want her to clean the hell out of the floors, dishes, kids' toys," I said. "Let's not risk more confusion."

Some cultural misalignments took months to figure out. Marc's cholesterol was through the roof at his stateside checkup after our first year in Delhi. When we were back in India after home leave, I asked Chote Lal how much butter and ghee were going into the delicious meals he made. "Madame, only using one kg. butter a week," he said with surprise. I slowly converted from metric: one kg. is slightly over two pounds of butter … and in a week!!

Margarine wasn't available on the Indian market, so I tapped my friend Lisa, who had commissary privileges, for regular margarine deliveries. When she dropped off the first plastic container, I pressed it on Chote Lal as convincingly as possible: "Please, no more butter or you'll kill *Sahib!*" I needed the hyperbole because I was making a really big ask; Chote Lal was justifiably proud of his cooking, and margarine was not going to perform up to his standards. But he wagged his head from side to side in the Indian way, took the margarine from my hand, and conceded defeat. Marc's cholesterol dropped back down by his next checkup.

Complaint: Flies

Flies were everywhere. Just talking to a friend on the street could bring fly trouble, as it did to my margarine provider. Lisa swallowed a fly as she walked down the street chatting with a neighbor. Within 24 hours, she was gut sick, and gut sick in Delhi means that incredible substances pour out of your body. You survive, but for several hours you wish you wouldn't. In our house, at the appearance of those uninvited guests, I focused like Jim Corbett tracking a man eater. I grabbed my fly swatter, stalked the bug, and squashed it. When Meera or Margaret caught sight of me, they'd call out, "Madame is hunting!"

Eventually I had my own icky encounter with flies, but at least I didn't swallow one. Our household help had first rights to anything we tossed out, the dividing up supervised by Chote Lal. By the time each took what was due them, only dregs were left to dump in the public dustbin near the back of our house; from us and our neighbors came nothing of value, only fruit pits and vegetable peelings, empty juice boxes and used disposable diapers. Wandering cows, sometimes with used disposable diapers stuck to their muzzles, browsed dustbins for food bits. One such cow breathed her last in the dustbin behind our house, and her carcass was left lying there in the sun.

Soon the screens on our back bedroom windows—the windows below which the kids' sandbox sat—were covered with flies. By "covered" I mean completely covered so that they looked like fuzzy blankets. Thousands of flies waited to take a turn on the cow's body; their buzzing produced an electric hum in our back rooms.

I was an inexperienced American with a big fly problem, and Marc was out of town. I did what I would have done in the States and took out the Delhi phonebook, checked municipal listings, found "Dead Animal Removal," called the number, and reported my problem. A prompt resolution was promised. I repeated that call twice daily for a week with no results as the cow rotted. Finally, Marc returned home. He knew by then that municipal bureaucracies do not solve problems in India; they create official documents, move them around, and provide jobs for part of the vast population. The power of politics, fueled by money and wielded in face-to-face encounters, was what solved problems. So, Marc showed up at the office of the neighborhood's Congress-I Party representative and laid out our situation. What was left of the cow was gone the next day, and the flies left.

Lynn Litterine

*A Feral Cow and Feral Pigs Snacking
at the Dustbin Near Our House*

Delight: Handcrafts

Indians make beautiful objects with their hands, and craftsmen seek to faithfully reproduce what craftsmen before them have made for centuries, maybe eons. Tradition is valued, not innovation. A country's crafts can say a lot about its people. The pieces I loved and bought opened doors to stories of Indian life. A large, heavy *ghara* (clay water jug) spoke of a village woman who walked miles between her hut and her water source every day. In the slow sway of her body as she walked with the *ghara* balanced on her head, I read patience and strength in the heat. The chime of tiny bells from an ankle bracelet mirrored the sound of Meera's laugh, girlish and flirtatious, as both the bells and her laughter were intended to be. Hand-carved blocks used to print textiles, especially the old blocks deeply stained with dye, took me into scenes where workers squatted over great lengths of cotton cloth and hand-stamped patterns on them.

The National Handicrafts and Handlooms Museum in Delhi is a treasure house. The most stunning piece I saw there was a length of hand-woven silk that looked like fabric made by elves or fairies, so light it might have floated up to the ceiling if the display case were opened. But even at the museum, most crafts were down-to-earth—toys, puppets for storytelling, clay figures, simple musical instruments. The grounds held changing exhibits of what Indian hands produced, and those exhibits let me wander the whole subcontinent without leaving Delhi. Traditionally built houses from 15 Indian states lined the walkways. I could watch an Orissan or Kashmiri artisan work in front of a traditional house from Orissa or Kashmir. Sometimes a whole show was the artisans and crafts in many media from one state; sometimes a show was artisans from all over the subcontinent in one medium—textiles, maybe, or metal or basketry.

Few objects were priced like fine art. Though the work was both fine and art, the Indians who made it took a matter-of-fact approach. I could afford the interesting things they made, so at the museum and with the *wallahs* on the street or at my door, I rarely bargained over prices, although I was expected to. I looked at the price with my western eye ("That is inexpensive for something so charming"), and the craftsman looked at the price with his Indian eye ("That is a lot more than I expected to get"). I had nothing to prove, so I paid their price, and we both left happy.

Marc Kaufman

Fired-Clay Statue of a Holy Man/ Bihar

I bought clay figures of holy men and nursing mothers from a Bihari craftsman at the museum. Some were sun-dried and the color of terra cotta; those fired in a kiln, like the holy man above, were black. My holy man is, I think, a Brahmin priest, not the wild-haired mendicant *saddhus* who came to our gate. Brahmins sit atop Hinduism's spiritual hierarchy. Some are wealthy, and some are not; some are even poor, but their high status is locked in at birth by being born into a Brahmin family. All the babies of the clay mothers were boys sporting tiny penises. A few lucky mothers were even nursing twin boys. Those boys were the greatly valued sons who would one day marry and bring both dowries and their brides' working hands into their families.

* * *

Marc Kaufman

Kavad Story-Telling Box / Rajasthan

As story tellers open the many doors on these boxes, they spin tales about the gods and demigods pictured on them, so the boxes are also called portable altars. The boxes, like India itself, teem with gods and goddesses and images from ancient stories. I think mine tells the epic of the *Ramayana* because the monkey god, Hanuman, and the 10-headed demon Ravana are depicted. When I hold the story box, I hold an entire epic narrative that, typical of India's blend of ancient and modern, was also on television during our stay. Unlike that serialized version on TV, all the characters are on display at once in the *kavad*. I live among their images, and I read their story as a child or an illiterate villager would.

* * *

The "Lace" Panels of a Hand-Carved Wooden Jalidahr Screen/Kashmir

The *naqqash* (master carver) who made this screen told me, "The young men don't want to do work like this anymore. It takes too long." Indeed. He had taken solid walnut wood and turned it into four lacey panels that were each six feet high. His level of skill took unimaginable patience to develop and unimaginable patience to exercise. But maybe, as an older Indian craftsman, his hands defined time's passage by the carving of the screen, not by a clock. How many hours did it take to correctly carve a screen like this? The number of hours that it took to correctly carve a screen like this. The clock wasn't his timekeeper; the screen was.

* * *

I collected textile blocks of all sizes. The clean, finely carved ones were displayed on curio shop shelves, but many of my blocks I dug out of wooden barrels on dusty shop floors. Some were carved in a design, and some were inlaid with thin strips of metal to create the design. Worn and stained with dye, they spoke of hard and constant labor and were probably used to print some of the cheap hippie bedspreads and dresses I bought in the '60s.

The most intricate block in my collection is pristine. I bought it at the yearly crafts fair in Surajkund, a scrubland park outside Delhi. The young man I bought it from, Abdul Qayyum, was from Farrukhabad in Uttar Pradesh. He carved the ornate design "to show off what I could do," he told me, and he had a right to show off; like my wooden screen, his carving turned hard wood into a lacelike pattern. The block has never pressed dye to cloth, but just once I made a print on paper of it in poster paint then gently scrubbed the block clean in deference to Abdul Qayyum.

Lynn Litterine
The Block Carved to Show Off What He Could Do
(6 ¾ inches wide by 6 ¼ inches tall / depth of carving 1/8 inch)

Marc Kaufman

Cutout Sculpture in Brass

I think this brass piece represents *Purusha*, a cosmic being described in the *Rig Veda* (probably composed between 1500 and 1200 BCE). All four classes of humanity (*varnas*) are said to have sprung from *Purusha's* body:

> The *varnas* have been known since a hymn in the *Rig Veda* (the oldest surviving Indian text) that portrays the *Brahman* (priest), the *Kshatriya* (noble), the *Vaishya* (commoner), and the *Shudra* (servant) issued forth at creation from the mouth, arms, thighs, and feet of the primeval person (*purusha*). (www.britannica.com/topic/varna-Hinduism)

I need to add that some experts think that reference in the *Rig Veda* is not original to the text. Classes and castes have been a source of both social stability and social conflict in India, of automatic privilege for some and automatic oppression for others; controversy is inevitable whenever they come up for discussion. I like the way the single flowing line of the silhouette could represent a reality so complex and so difficult for so many millions of Indians over so many centuries. Its simple line speaks to layers of history, religion, and conflict.

* * *

Because prices weren't steep, I usually bought whatever handcrafts I wanted, but not always. The most beautiful object I brought home with me is a memory of something I didn't buy. It was a small bell cast in silver and gold with an incised design of tiny flowers. Lovely to look at, but its great beauty was its sound. When it rang as I lifted it off the shop counter, the air around me shimmered. I wanted so much to hear that sound every day of my life. It cost more than I could spend, so I left the shop without it. But maybe not completely without it because I've just shared it here.

Complaint: A Rat in My Home

I like animals, but a creature showed up in my New Delhi home that I was deeply un-thrilled to see. The afternoon it visited, the house was quiet. The staff was on lunch break, and John had snoozed off next to me on his sleep mat on the floor. I was deciding whether to sink into a nap with him or to get some things done when I heard a metallic rattling from the guest bathroom. I went to check, but as I peered around the doorframe, the rattling stopped. I'd interrupted something. The drain cover in the shower was up and slightly tilted, and it took me a moment to register that it rested on the head of a big sewer rat. The rat and I both squeaked, and I slammed the bathroom door shut and locked it. Silly, but my toddler was sleeping on the floor not far away. Then, as if the rat were armed with a battering ram, I sat with my back against the door until Chote Lal returned from lunch and a nap or card game or whatever they were up to in Ram's quarters. Chote Lal took immediate action. He went to the market, bought a small bag of cement and a trowel, and, when he returned, shooed me away from the bathroom door, which I was still guarding. He cemented the drain cover solidly in place as I checked the drain covers in Dave's bathroom and ours. They were snug; the builders had missed only one.

Delight: Other Fauna

Some animals I welcomed. The beige gecko that moved into our house even before we did was the closest thing we had to a pet. I named him Barney, and he mostly kept to himself. I saw him twice a day when I opened and closed the dining-room drapes and he fell out of the drapes onto the floor. Plop! His small self always seemed fine; after the plunge, he skittered off and climbed back up the drapes to fall off again the next time the cord was pulled.

I saw striking birds that were new to me--not that a lizard in the drapes wasn't new for me. My favorite birds were the small green parrots (*totas*) who cruised the neighborhood in noisy groups like kids. I liked spotting hoopoes, too, because their plumage is so startling. They have zebra-striped wings and tail and a rosy-brown body, but their most dramatic feature is a tall "crown" of those same rosy-brown feathers, each one tipped in black and white.

And I liked seeing fruit bats. Dark-furred and lanky with big ears and long, thin snouts, they looked like Ichabod Cranes hung upside down from tree branches. A great many of the two-foot-long bats rested in trees outside the Ashok Hotel in Chanakyapuri, a fancy Delhi neighborhood. Headed for a spicy lunch at the Ashok's South Indian restaurant, I might see several dozens of them hanging from their claws. I supposed they flew at night to search for fruit, but I never saw one fly, so I can't say if they had the five-and-a-half-foot wingspan some fruit bats unfurl.

Complaint: Quality (Out of) Control

Consumer goods and services seesawed wildly in reliability; quality control presented a real problem. For instance, getting phones installed and using them successfully required colossal patience. Even express handling of phone installations for the wealthy, the powerful, and foreigners could take months. For a middle-class Indian, it could take years to get a line. And once the line was installed, service was irregular. Calls sometimes ended mid-sentence and could not be reconnected. Or a dialed number would only produce an operator yelling *"Hanji? Hanji? Yes? Yes?"* over and over. Service was so bad that, shortly before we moved to India, a frustrated government minister stormed the central telephone exchange waving a gun. No one was hurt, no charges were filed, and the minister became something of a folk hero across Delhi.

Electricity was also a work in progress. After the early fire in our meter board, nothing more burst into flames, but the flow of electricity was erratic. That wasn't alarming when the current dipped, the lights dimmed, and the big air conditioner units set in the walls shivered and groaned. But a spike in the current was scary. Ceiling fans spun like meat-cutter blades. Lightbulbs blazed. Air conditioners revved up to a squeal. Eventually, the current dropped back down again, sometimes even to normal.

The quality of goods ranged widely. An example: Chote Lal made a great tuna-fish salad sandwich. The only variable in his sure-fire recipe was how much roe was packed into the tuna fish can at processing. Sometimes half the can or more was filled with fish eggs; sometimes there were none. The eggs looked odd and tasted too rich in sandwiches, but they didn't make us sick, and we learned to eat them. Personal-care products weren't under complete control either. One Delhi entrepreneur sold a line of high-end skin creams, and her facial moisturizer was mild enough for my dry skin. The cooling pink cream wasn't loaded with strong fragrance like some Indian cosmetics. I used it for all three years in India in spite of the occasional jar that turned my face pink—and not in a good way. And, under quality control, I'll also mention Indian disposable diapers, the ones Dave called "explodable diapers," which said it all.

Delight: A Low-Tech Approach

Many Indian crafts were produced so simply that the process itself was elegant. Clay pots, for instance, baked only by the sun or in a temporary kiln made of more clay, fueled with dried cow dung, lit, sealed, then broken apart to get the pots when a gut instinct told the potter the time was right—no temperature dial, no timer. Objects made that way had a casual charm. The low-tech approach was widely applied: laborers walked to work chewing neem twigs to clean their teeth; car repairmen squatted on the ground amid piles of used parts; a carpenter built a wooden slide for my sons and lined it with shiny black particleboard; construction workers lashed bamboo poles together with rope for scaffolding to build even the tallest buildings downtown. And truly dreamlike, on late nights after dinner parties, while we drove home on the foggy Ring Road, flatbed trailers suddenly appeared ahead loaded with steel I-beams and pulled by six ghostly Brahma bullocks leaning into their yokes.

I knew that hard-working Indians might have preferred convenience and ease. Big stores full of affordable stuff for the house or big one-stop groceries, lightweight plastic buckets instead of heavy clay water jugs, a computerized workplace instead of hundreds of paper files tied with ribbons. I hoped their lives and work would get easier. But I also knew that their skills and simple self-sufficiency had a dignity and strength I'd never sensed at a big-box store. On home leave, I walked the aisles of chain drugstores where the array of clear shampoos alone was so overwhelming, I couldn't come up with a reason to buy any specific one. All I needed to do was wash my hair, but I was faced with complex shampoo formulas, each claiming to be unique. I missed the simplicity of India.

Complaint: Heat, Of Course

New Delhi sits in a semi-arid plain, and its highest hot season temperatures after we arrived in 1987 were 98.96 dry degrees on June 26 and 28, 101.12 dry degrees on June 29, and 98.42 dry degrees on July 2. The monsoon rains failed, and Delhi baked in the sun. For weeks, temperatures didn't leave the 90s except to hit the 100s. In Delhi's ambient heat, my mind went blank and my body lost any sense of a boundary between it and the surrounding heat. The water in the ACSA pool felt like pee, and I couldn't feel a difference between the air conditioner exhaust and the ambient air as I walked up our driveway. Even night temperatures crept near 90 degrees. I did not like being one with that heat.

And hot season temperatures required some attention. On a day shortly after we moved in, I spent a lot of time unpacking and organizing our things, and my feet were sore once I'd finished. Of course, I thought, I've been standing and moving around on them all day; I haven't sat down once. I haven't even sat down on the toilet! How could that be? I had guzzled water, soda, limeade, and tea all day, and in spite of being indoors with the air conditioners on, I had not needed to pee. I had stayed hydrated, but only just.

And a hot season without monsoon rains, like our first one, means that farm crops are parched and need increased irrigation, so water and the electricity to pump it are diverted to that greater good. Residential supplies dipped to almost nothing that hot season, and when water wasn't running in our pipes and electricity wasn't running through our wires, our faucets ran dry and even our brick and masonry house heated up. The boys, Meera, and I once decamped to a hotel, but most Indians had no such option. They helped each other along with big clay jugs of water left in front of their houses and businesses for passers-by to drink from. I didn't know real dry heat before India; since then, summer's humid heat in Maryland has felt soft and luxurious.

Delight: Food

Lychees with papery rosy skin and an ebony bead of a pit in the middle of silky white flesh. I could eat a kg. of them in an evening in front of the TV. Mangoes in as many varieties as American apples and subjects of the same folk tales in which kids steal and eat so many unripe ones that their stomachs ache. Custard apples, shaped like fat pine cones with rough, pale-green, skin. Split open, the creamy white flesh justifies the word "custard" in flavor and consistency. Apples from the Kulu Valley, small and far from picture perfect but tasting like freshly squeezed cider. Each fruit arrived only in its own season, which made it an object of desire. To crave a custard apple that wouldn't show up for months, and later, finally, to have one in hand felt like I'd been given a small gift. Indian winter carrots, bright red like tomatoes. Uncooked, they are juicy and sweet, but when made into *gajar ka halwah*, a cooked dessert of winter carrots, ghee, cardamom seeds, milk, and nuts, nothing short of heavenly. And, as if the *halwah* isn't already pretty enough, most cooks decorate it with wispy bits of edible silver or gold leaf. I found a tea from the Nilgiri Hills that was full of flavor but with no sharp edges, perfect for *masala chai,* the spiced tea served across India in what must be millions of gallons a day.

Some of my pleasure in food came from appreciating the challenges Chote Lal conquered when he cooked. I grew up eating Italian food, and I can say with authority that his water buffalo lasagna was primo. When

John or Dave asked for a birthday cake shaped like a skateboard or an elephant, Chote Lal produced one that looked spot on, was springy and moist, and was iced with butter-cream frosting. And he made a tuna casserole that was up to church-supper standards. Our friend Carol, who also made a great one, certified that when she visited.

India didn't produce many beers, and most of them tasted like chemicals, even the popular Kalyani Black Label and Kingfisher that are sold in the States now in what *must* be different formulas. Nothing suited me in the heat but a cold Rosy Pelican, a lager with full flavor and no industrial aftertaste. Sometimes I had to settle for a case of the B-team brews; even their labels paled next to the one with the fat pink pelican on it.

The weirdest thing that went into my mouth while I was in India was *paan*. *Paan* isn't eaten; it's something to chew on and enjoy the taste of, like gum. It produces what britannica.com characterizes as a "copious flow of brick-red saliva" that Indians spit out everywhere. Its color is so robust that spit stains left by the workers who built our house were permanently part of the composite stone floors. Near the end of our stay, I asked Jai Singh to buy some *paan* for me; I had to try it. As the household watched, I popped what looked like a short green cigar and smelled of spice and rose petals into my mouth and began to chew. Britannica.com explains that betel nuts, an ingredient of *paan,* contain something called "inferior catechu," which in turn contains an alkaloid used by veterinarians to worm animals, and, while chewing the *paan,* I felt like I was being wormed. As the *paan* kicked in, not only did my mouth flood with saliva, but the lining of my throat stiffened as if it might swell closed completely. Whether that was due to the slaked lime ("caustic lime" is another name for it) also in the *paan* or to the astringent catechu, which can be used to tan leather, I don't know. Too inhibited to spit on the floor, I tried to keep up with all the spit by swallowing. As my throat tightened, I told myself that millions of Indian *paan* chewers weren't choking to death in the streets and neither would I. When the tight sensation eased after a couple of minutes, I looked up at my household staff; everyone was making a sincere effort not to laugh.

Complaint: Poop

I have no delicate way to put this complaint. Poop from humans and animals was all over the place, and it got on my nerves. I might have anticipated it and not entered the public toilets piled high with poop in Lodhi Garden, but I didn't. I might have walked past pig poop on the way to Dave's school bus often enough to become inured, but I didn't. I might have ignored it on the path when Marc and I took an evening stroll through acacia woods near our house, but I didn't. I might have looked past it at the pretty stream we stopped by when the car broke down in Punjab, but I didn't. And after a visit with the Dalai Lama, I might have been self-realized enough to not notice it on a trail lined with wild rhododendrons in the Himalayan foothills, but, alas, I wasn't. A bigger person might have gotten over it. I was not big enough. I never did.

Delight: Books

Books have always been a delight, and India was full of books. Bookstores were packed with inexpensive volumes from all over the world, the rare imports to India that weren't heavily taxed. I was told that Jawaharlal Nehru insisted on a low book tax to foster literacy and education, but I have never been able to confirm that. India also had its own robust publishing industry, often in partnership with British publishing houses.

In my three years there, every book I read was about India, and I enjoyed them all: *Freedom At Midnight* by Larry Collins and Dominique Lapierre, *City Of Joy* by Dominque Lapierre, *The Room on the Roof* by Ruskin Bond, *Untouchable* by Mulk Raj Anand, *Third-class Ticket* by Heather Wood, *An Indian Attachment* by Sarah Lloyd, *Plain Tales from the Hills* by Rudyard Kipling, *Train to Pakistan* by Khushwant Singh, *An Area of Darkness* by V.S. Naipaul, *Midnight's Children* by Salman Rushdie, *Indian Folk Art* by Heinz Mode and Subodh Chandra, *The Warlis: Tribal Paintings and Legends* Jivya Soma Mashe, Bali Mashe, and Lakshmi Lal, *National Handicrafts and Handlooms Museum* by Jyotindra Jain and Aarti Aggarwalla. So many books, my introvert's way of trying to understand the people around me.

Two books by Sudhir Kakar, an Indian psychoanalyst trained in the west, shaped some of that understanding. Although his career has been controversial, I found that *Shamans, Mystics, and Doctors* (The University of Chicago Press, 1982) gave me insights into Indian versus western ideas about illness and cure. Those insights helped me work with how the people in my household approached medicine. When Meera had some kind of "female trouble" and would only speak with and not undress to be examined by the doctor we went to, a woman, or when someone explained an illness by "my bad luck," I could understand the context, even if I didn't agree. But Kakar's most useful book for me was *The Inner World: A Psycho-analytic Study of Childhood and Society in India* (Oxford University India Perennials, 1978). Near the end of our three years in India, I faced a sudden conflict between two people in my household, and Kakar helped me make sense of what might have been going on. More on that later.

Dave had books at his school library, and I'd brought children's books for John from the States. But John's books reflected none of the reality that surrounded him every day—none of the clothes, none of the food, none of the animals. Then I discovered the Children's Book Trust, a publisher in Delhi founded in 1957 by K. Shankar Pillai,

> "to promote the production of well written, well illustrated and well designed books for children. In furtherance of this objective, the Trust brings out books that are easy to read and easy on the eyes, including books that enable children to have a better appreciation of India's cultural heritage."
> (www.chidlrensbooktrust.com)

Perfect! And they were priced reasonably, which was nice for me but especially helpful to Indian families who were not affluent. These were some of John's favorites:

Written by Alaka Shankar
Illustrated by Jagdish Joshi
Published by Children's Book Trust, 1976

In *Sonali's Friend*, a toddler likes to watch the crow in her yard, a gray and black hooded crow like the ones in our Delhi neighborhood. She calls out to it, "Kaa kaa," whenever she sees it. "*Koa*" (crow) was one of John's first words in Hindi, which made sense because the crows were big and loud and showed up everywhere he went. When the crow steals Sonali's cookie, the theft was familiar, too. John had seen Koa snatch a whole bag of potato chips from a child at ACSA.

Written by Rupa Gupta
Illustrated by Samuel [sic/one name]
Published by Children's Book Trust, 1987

In *Lali and Bablu's Mango Tree,* characters look like the people John saw on the streets of Delhi. Even better, the book is about his favorite Indian fruit. Lali and Bablu's grandparents plan to cut down the mango tree in their yard because it hasn't been fruiting, and money has been offered for its wood. But the children love the tree, so Lali and Bablu sell a stool they've made and use the money to play a trick on their grandparents. Twice they buy mangos and scatter them beneath the tree to make it look like it has fruited, but they scatter two different kinds of mangos— *langras* and *dusehris.* Grandpa sees through the trick, as John would have, too, because like Grandpa, he knew a *dusehri*, his favorite kind of mango, when he saw one.

Written by Surekha Panandiker
Illustrated by Mrinal Mitra
Published by Children's Book Trust, 1984

In *Chitku*, a young mouse by that name cannot stay out of trouble because he loves *laddus*, an Indian sweet that John also loved. Chitku steals *laddus*, which makes the people in his house angry, and they adopt a cat to solve the problem. When the mouse and the cat meet face to face in the family storeroom, a wild chase follows during which Chitku knocks over a tin of spice, and the powder covers his tail. Things look grim for the little mouse as the cat clamps a paw down on his back. But when Chitku flicks his tail, spice hits the cat's nose and triggers a sneezing fit. "'Aakchee! Aakchee!'" the cat sneezes, and Chitku escapes.

Delight: Cow Dust Hour

This time of day begins as the sun starts to set. The light outdoors slides from white—a brutal white in hot season—to a rosy apricot. In village India, at that hour, the cows come back from grazing. Their hooves kick up ancient dust as they plod home, and that gives "cow dust hour" its name. As the work day wound down across India, mine did, too. Ahead of me was supper, the boys' baths, and some cozy reading to each of them in bed. Cow dust hour was a collective sigh by the whole country, and I joined in.

Friends Were Needed

Few of my friendships were with Indians, not by my choosing but by my circumstances. My women friends were met, as they'd been met stateside, through the boys' activities. Since John's playgroup was run American style (moms and kids, but no *ayahs*), we attracted westerners. And India did not allow Indian families to attend AES, so volunteering at Dave's school didn't put me in touch with Indian parents either. Another way of making Indian friends was through work, but Marc's work took him all over South and Southeast Asia. His associates in Delhi were foreign journalists.

So, my friendships were with westerners, and most of them entered our lives early and brought their spouses with them. Laura, the wife of an American journalist, began writing to me and answering my questions while I was still in the States. As Laura's letters with suggestions arrived, I stockpiled a mound of supplies to ship. Mosquito nets. Cloth diapers. Sturdy clothes. Liquid anti-malarials. Extra sippy cups. We overlapped in Delhi for only a year, but friendships deepened fast between women who had kids and traveling husbands; we depended on each other. When Laura began miscarrying while our husbands were in Pakistan, she didn't want to be alone. So she moved into our house with her daughter and *ayah* until her husband could get back and take her to Bangkok for treatment.

* * *

Another close friendship bloomed through Marc's time in the customs shed at the airport. The tall man behind him in line was American, and they chatted as they waited in the heat for their household goods to clear. Customs agents spread out our shipment on the floor and closely examined each item. We'd bought a Fisher-Price tape player for John and forgotten to make its box look used by beating it up a bit. The agents pounced on it. Pristine electronics! Customs duties due! Marc never offered *baksheesh* (bribes), so he was told to come back the next day to pay the tax. Why the next day? For the sheer inconvenience of it.

His new pal worked for the U.S. Department of Defense and lived on the American compound, so his goods sailed through barely inspected and definitely untaxed. But, he confided to Marc, he had his gun collection with him and was nervous that it might create a problem, but he had planned ahead. He pre-emptively handed a bottle of good Scotch to the customs agent before the carton of guns was opened. The agent cast an indifferent glance at the sealed carton and moved it along.

I met that American a few days later at the ACSA pool when he walked over to us and set down a huge box of American disposable diapers from the commissary. "Take it," he said and went back to sit with his wife and kids. At customs, Marc had told him Dave's joke about "Indian explodables."

For all three years we knew him, Marc suspected that our friend worked in intelligence, but he never asked. Marc was regularly in Afghanistan covering the Afghan-Soviet War and in Kashmir covering border conflicts among India, Pakistan, and China. After a reporting trip, our friend was always full of questions about what Marc had seen. The last time we got together before our family came home for good, Marc could resist no longer. "I want to ask you a delicate question about your work," he said. Our friend didn't miss a beat. "Yes, I am," he answered. And the subject was dropped.

* * *

By great good luck, the first mom I met at the ACSA kiddie pool was that wife of the pediatrician with CARE. She had twins John's age and a boy about two years older. Carmen was both a good person and a strong, grounded woman. She had breastfed her twins through her own bout of dengue fever in Bangladesh, so she was tough, but she was also warm and kind, a woman who never criticized anyone who didn't richly deserve it. She wanted to be in India, and when I was with her, I remembered why I wanted to be there.

* * *

My margarine and Nestle's Quik supplier was a friend who lived down the street. She and her husband, Tom, who worked on water projects for USAID, were from Minnesota. Unlike me, Lisa's strongest exclamation when faced with a problem was "gol" (short for "golly"). She made me think of daisies and black-eyed susans.

Most people brought a few favorite possessions from home to their postings in Delhi. Mine were two of my mom's Santa Claus figures—the first one she'd bought and the last I'd given her before she died. Tom's piece of home was a model train set big enough to cover a ping-pong table, which he also brought. Whenever my kids walked in his door, he'd get his tiny railroad running for them. But Delhi is a dusty place, and dust messes with the contact between model trains and their tracks. Tom's railroad never ran for more than a couple of minutes in a row, but the kids seemed happy enough with that.

* * *

My English friend Deborah decided to introduce herself when she heard me snuffling at a winter-holiday program at AES. South Korean students in traditional dress were singing, I think *Jingle Bells*, and I was happy-crying in my we-are-the-world moment. Deborah also was moved by that good feeling and figured the snuffling woman she heard nearby might be a fit as a friend. That was my good luck because she helped me at a low point that came later in India and also because she is still a wise and loving friend.

Deborah, like Carmen and Harriet, did not give in to germs. She was an inveterate traveler to interesting, unhygienic places. On many weekends in India, her family packed up their van and off they'd go with their four little boys, one an infant born in Delhi, somewhere, anywhere, with notable animals or important cultural sites. After some of those weekends, having eaten or drunk something questionable on the road, Deborah was crouched over her toilet back in Delhi. Recovered by even the following weekend, off she'd go again. I am trying hard not to use the phrase "stiff upper lip" here.

Letter Home to an Old Friend
One Year and Two Months In

August 23, 1988

Dear Diane,

We're back from 6 weeks' vacation in Hong Kong, Berkeley (Adele's), Philadelphia and East Hampton (Marc's folks). Back to mold, flies, stink, cholera, conjunctivitis, earthquakes. John's been to the doctor twice in the 21 days since we landed. School's been open 2 weeks, and David's already missed a day sick. My attitude is not particularly positive this year. Unlike last August, this year I can see the whole year stretching before me, and I'm aware of all the unpleasant, tiresome things it will present. I have 10 months to go, and I'm exhausted already. Marc left 6 days after our return and will be away almost 3 weeks—Burma and Pakistan. I find single parenting very draining, especially with a 2 1/2-year-old. So, we're back, I'm depressed, and you're getting a stinky letter. ... John and I are in a more American-style playgroup this year. Last year, everyone but me came with their ayahs. All the mothers sat in the living room talking and drinking coffee. All the ayahs were in the playroom with the kids. It made for a nice grownup visit, but no chance at all to see my kid interact. Mostly, the kids played with their [own] ayahs. This year it's [just] mothers and kids, and we're trying to introduce a couple of short, structured activities for each session ... we're doing a little story circle, some songs, cleaning up together (the little sahibs and missy babas have casts of thousands to pick up after them at home), maybe a little art as they get bigger ... I came back to India with 3 newspaper stories to do ... I don't feel like me if I don't do some writing ... I've also stepped-up volunteer work with Home and School and with the American Women's Assn. I'm hoping to do more cultural stuff this year, more dance, music, art galleries, and however much traveling we can afford (Nepal and Everest, I hope; a swing through Rajasthan with a friend who's coming in Feb.) Our 2 regular saddhus have been through already, greeted and smeared me and John with sandal paste. The year begins. Love, Lynn

The Boys' Lives

Dave and John met their friends in classes at AES and at the ACSA pool. From our first days in New Delhi to our last, the school and the club made life easier for the kids and me.

Although AES had teachers from many countries, including India, its curriculum and approach were American and seamlessly familiar to us. By-rote learning was not practiced; students' creativity was encouraged; students were treated as individual learners whenever possible. But the school was firmly rooted in India, too. Art classes included Indian media and themes. A re-enactment of the story of the god Ram was put on every year by the elementary school. Hindi was available in the upper grades. And older AES students ran a community service project for children from a nearby slum. That after-school gathering might do arts and crafts projects but was just as likely to shampoo the kids' hair.

ACSA was on the embassy's residential campus, and the pool was open for all of hot season and short parts of both cool and monsoon seasons. The clubhouse had a sit-down restaurant, where we had dinner on Sundays, when most families' cooks were off. A flaming, sizzling, popping steak on a metal platter was the favorite dinner choice. Was it beef or buff (water buffalo)? Sometimes Indian officials took a-wink-and-a-nod approach toward the law when it involved foreigners, and I guess we were on American soil at the club, but I'd bet on buff because the taboo against killing cattle is so strong. Beef or buff, the steaks were good. The clubhouse also had a small café-and-store that sold hamburgers (again, beef or buff?), hotdogs, and American candy.

The Little League field at the club was where Dave made the transition from picking his nose in the outfield in second grade to being on the championship team in fourth grade. John and I watched from the bleachers, some American candy in John's hand and some spiced tea in mine. Except that the League's power hitter was a young Indian girl dressed in traditional *salwar kameez*—her parents worked on the compound— we could have been in an American suburb, a feeling intensified by the sweet smell of cut grass that drifted over from the lawn on the residential part of the compound.

The women's hiring exchange, where I had my first meltdown, was on club grounds, too, along with the embassy commissary. The commissary was for military and embassy employees and contractors only, but we were allowed to check out videos there. Chote Lal developed quite a crush on Miss Yvonne, the Most Beautiful Woman in Puppet Land on *Pee Wee's Playhouse*. He never said a word but would slip from the kitchen into the living room whenever the boys were watching a video of the show and Pee Wee announced the arrival of bouffant-coiffed Miss Yvonne. He would stand behind their chairs smiling happily until Miss Yvonne and her ample endowments left the screen; at which time, he'd return to his kitchen.

We did get a little more than videos from the commissary but not officially. That friend who bought margarine for us also made sure that David had Nestle's Quik because Cadbury's Drinking Chocolate, the only one available at local markets, was chalky and didn't make the cut with Dave.

* * *

So, AES and ACSA were places where David and John could get a little taste of America. John was young enough not to miss the States; wherever his mom, dad, and big brother were was home to him. But David remembered the snacks, toys, and pals he'd left behind. That same good friend who had commissary privileges would bring him Cheese Balls on his birthday, and the Snickers we bought at the ACSA cafe helped, too. But Dave's big American candy grab came each Halloween, when some houses on the American compound opened for trick or treat. Households that had stocked up on sweets at the commissary were decorated to identify them for the trick-or-treating children of ACSA members. At dusk, house lights winked on as the children crisscrossed the lawn in the center of the compound. Listening to kids' excited calls to each other felt like Halloween at home. Only the mid-80s temperature was different.

Lynn Litterine

David Ready to Plunder the American Embassy Compound for Candy

Western holidays were improvisational in India; the traditional supplies weren't available. But those incongruities were lost on John. He remembered nothing from stateside holidays. ACSA did a Christmas celebration in December during which Santa arrived on an elephant (*hathi* in Hindi), and children were handed up to ride with him. John's first time at that celebration, he enjoyed the ride, but the big news as far as he was concerned was what happened when Santa and the elephant entered the compound gate. John was quick to tell Meera about it when we got home. He was still having trouble pronouncing –s, so the news came out this way: "Meemee, Hanta come onna *hathi*, and *hathi* make a biiiiig pee-pee." Indeed, the elephant peed hugely when it entered the gate, and moms, dads, and kids jumped back to get out of the splash.

Unlike his brother, David noticed the changes we made as we navigated between cultures. As early as September, he asked me, "Should I leave *lassi* and *gulab jamun* for Santa this year?" Of course! So, at our house, Santa drank sugared yoghurt water and ate fried balls of milk powder in syrup on Christmas Eve. Carrots for the reindeer (and the Easter bunny) remained the same as stateside.

That first Christmas, I bypassed the scraggly Christmas trees sold on Delhi streets. Much of India was deforested, and a tree grown and cut down just for our holiday use seemed selfish, so I bought a potted evergreen that we could replant later in the garden. Its shape was good; it was about five feet high in its pot; it held enough decorations to look Christmas-y. That tree suited us so well, we bought little potted trees for all three Christmases and added them to the garden after the holidays.

Marc Kaufman

Potted Christmas Trees

The boys, like most kids, were usually unyielding conservatives about family holiday traditions, but they enjoyed our Christmas trees in India so much that we dragged quirky little trees in from our backyard for several years after we came back to the States.

Rides on horses, camels, and elephants at birthday parties and on holidays and visits to forest parks were fun for John and David, but elephants were always the clear favorites. The creatures were so large, so prettily decorated with flower patterns in colorful powders, and, when under the control of their *mahouts* (keepers), so sweet, slow, and gentle. Camels were okay with the kids, too, but not with me. Although the camels' faces were cute and their long eyelashes gorgeous, their breath stunk, and the rolling of those metaphorical ships of the desert made me seasick. But Marc and Dave were immune to motion sickness, and they enjoyed riding a camel that showed up at our front gate with his driver on our first Christmas.

Lynn Litterine

David and Marc Start a Christmas Camel Ride

John's World

Only 15 months old, John took to India on Day 1. He accepted his life there as normal. And that life was very good, especially at home. Did he want to dance? Four or five people in the household would grab his rhythm band instruments, make a circle around him, and play sticks, tambourines, and small drums for as long as John wanted to caper around the playroom. Their instinct was always to make him smile, although I eventually convinced at least Meera to set limits for him. Limit setting didn't interest the others; to them he was "*Chote Sahib*" (Little Sir) or "*Johnny-ji*" or "*Babu-ji*," terms of respect for adults that were affectionately applied to John, who was not yet three feet tall.

I have only a few photos of John looking cranky in India, but two of them were taken with Tibetan Buddhists, really among the loveliest of people. Really! The background to the first photo was India's heavy tax on goods from overseas. Western toys were snatched up when offered for resale, and I'd scored a used Big Wheel for John. He loved it and ended most days with a bath then a race around the playroom on his Big Wheel as the staff clapped and cheered, "Naked motorcycle driver! Naked motorcycle driver!"

Early in our posting, Marc did a story about a little Spanish boy who was identified by Tibetan Buddhists as a reincarnated lama. The child was living in Delhi. "He and John are about the same age," Marc said. "Maybe they'd enjoy playing together." A play date at a park was arranged—their first and their last. Osel, the little lama, really liked riding the Big Wheel, and John really didn't like sharing it. I resisted John's whining. How could I wrestle a toy away from a reincarnated lama? By the time Osel surrendered the Big Wheel, John was completely put out. Maybe that's why he walked out on the Dalai Lama two years later.

Marc Kaufman

John, Osel, and I on the Play Date

That unspeakable snub occurred in 1990, when Marc booked an interview in Dharamsala with the exiled leader of Tibet. Tibetans were, if possible, even more indulgent toward children than Indians were, so the boys were welcome at the interview. And no way was I going to miss a chance to meet him, so we all went with Marc to the compound where he lived. The Dalai Lama spent as much time with a visitor as he thought the visitor needed. Punctuality suffered, so we were ushered from the waiting room into the reception room an hour or two later than scheduled. That was a long time for a 3-year-old to wait. David held steady, but John was bored and restless. At first the adults chatted, then Marc began his interview. Soon, John put his mouth close to my ear and hissed, "I want to go now." He hissed that over and over into my ear until I lost track of everything the Dalai Lama said. Clearly, John and I had to leave. At least I'd met the Dalai Lama, but I wanted one more thing.

"Excuse me, your holiness, I need to take John back to the guesthouse now. Could we get a photo with you before he and I leave?"

In the photo, the Dalai Lama holds John's and David's hands and smiles like a realized being. David looks appropriately serious; Marc and I have tense smiles. And John? John is scowling.

Dalai Lama's Staff
"I want to go now. I want to go NOW!"

After John and I left, the Dalai Lama seemed taken aback. "Children usually respond well to me," he said.

John's now 39, and to this day we tease him about the bad karma he took on by walking out on the Dalai Lama. His annoyance with Osel was one thing; a favorite toy is hard to share when you're little. But turning his back on the current incarnation of Chenrezig, the bodhisattva of compassion? That was playing fast and loose, and John's still a bit uncomfortable about it.

Lynn Litterine

Birthday Cheese Puffs and a Chocolate Hathi Cake

(from a journal I kept for John) *"Here you are at 3, wearing a dhoti and kurta from Meera. We've hired a white horse for rides for your party guests. Our road is lined with policemen holding automatic rifles on the roofs because Yasir Arafat is at PLO headquarters down the street. Kinda scary."* A different kind of birthday, but John and his guests didn't notice.

Dave's World

The move to India was harder on David. He had a kid life in Philadelphia, his school, his friends, his favorite places to go. When he came down with chicken pox a week or so before our move, it was like rubbing salt into, well, chicken pox sores. His goodbye visits with friends were cancelled. He felt sick and itchy. His furniture was gone. His parents were frazzled. His last meal in the home he had come to at under a year old was Mickey D's on the floor of his empty bedroom. Dave remembered what he'd given up, and when he got to Delhi, he did not, like some of his classmates, live on the suburban facsimile that was the American compound. He did not get American food from the commissary. Initially, he had no playmates. Within a week, his father left on assignment. And all along, Dave's bright red hair triggered the open-mouthed stare at anything unusual that was common among Indians. David disliked being noticed for something he didn't control and he hated being stared at. We asked a lot of David.

In a journal I kept about him, I wrote on July 6, 1987,

> "India is hard so far. Too hot (up to well over 100 degrees) to play outdoors. No toys for 3 weeks+ awaiting our shipment. No school. Parents very miserable. Dave is working so hard to help. Boredom sometimes brings bad behavior. A few weeping sessions and 'I want to go home.' But so much staunch cheer, too. We have packed and moved 8x [in and out] since 6/23 because of problems at our house. One afternoon, Dave asked, 'Where did I wake up today?'"

The household staff surrounded Dave with kindness. In that same journal, I noted their gifts to Dave on his 7th birthday: a sweater from Meera, chocolates from Jai Singh, roses from Margaret, a soccer ball from Chote Lal, and a cricket set from Ram. And they decked Dave, John, and me in marigold necklaces (*malas*).

> "Dave had fun acting crazy. But later, he was feeling sad, and he was confused by feeling sad on his birthday.

'Even though it's my birthday and people were real nice to me at school and let me budge in all day, I still feel sad,' he told me.

"I felt sad about it myself. We meant this to be an adventure, something positive for him, and I feel instead that we've simply saddened our old Good Time Charlie, banked his fires, poor Boo."

And Dave couldn't help but pick up on my worries and meltdowns, which must have been hard in a place that was strange to him, where a bunch of other people pretty much lived with us full time, and where his father, his less mercurial parent, frequently was not home.

Dave was especially close to Marc, so being separated was hard. In his third-grade journal, he wrote, "[Rain] makes me feel sad because it's always darch [sic] and skcary [sic]. And I also feel like I'm in a spaceship fling [sic] throw [sic] space. My dad is in Thailand and I got a telex."

And some months later, "If I become a father I will never go to New Delhi with my faimly [sic] ... or go away for more then [sic] 3 weeks."

Dave hit his nadir in third grade on a trip we all took together. The four of us had a fun journey to Nepal. Dave saw the sun rise over the Himalayas, visited the monkey temple Swayambhunath, ate Tibetan dumplings, and saw Everest from a sightseeing plane. Afterward, Marc had stories to report in Nepal, so the boys and I flew back to Delhi without him. Takeoff out of the Kathmandu Valley is a nail biter, a steep, fast climb to avoid the surrounding peaks, but our plane had already leveled off when Dave suddenly yelled: "My dad's gonna die. I'll never see my dad again."

He was sobbing as he yelled, and I couldn't comfort him no matter what I tried. As time passed, Dave's wailing continued, and passengers were clearing their throats and shifting in their seats with impatience or nerves. Then a little boy appeared in the aisle at David's elbow. Wordlessly he handed Dave a toy truck and went back to his seat. Dave's screaming ratcheted down to sobbing then sniffling, and, finally, he was quiet and calm. I don't think the truck was what helped him; he already loved to play complicated computer games. I think the boy's simple, silent kindness calmed my son. Sometimes, when the world seems threatening, it helps to know that strangers can be kind. Or maybe the boy's appearance at his seat brought Dave back to their shared kids' world apart from the world of stressed-out grownups.

Marc and *David at Lodhi Garden*

"Living in India is hard," Dave wrote in his third-grade journal. "It is hard because you have to do a lot of stufe [sic] different from what you do in the States. It is also hard because it is very hot. And the pool hasn't opened yet. It is even harder than that because almost no one understands English [not true, but how Dave felt]. And because school gets out at 3:30."

And he wrote that he missed snow. Then, probably on his teacher's direction, he lists why India is fun: you can buy balloons off the street, go to the pool every day (once it re-opens), and on weekends go to ACSA and have a Twix. Balloons and Twix were thin gruel compared to home, but Dave always rose to the challenge of a school assignment.

Dave At School

David did second, third, and fourth grades at AES, which ran from the nursery school that John attended our last year through an International Baccalaureate year after high school. Dave's classmates and teachers came from all over the world, and he negotiated cultural differences every day. Only a third of the students were American, and some of those had been born in the States to parents whose citizenships were in other countries. The other two-thirds were "third country nationals," neither Americans nor Indians. In fact, Indian children couldn't attend the school. During a period of rocky relations with the United States, India had put AES off limits for its children.

As parents in diplomacy, development, and business moved on to new posts, losing friends was a frequent occurrence. The hardest loss for Dave was Louis, a French-Canadian boy and a true soul mate. And by "soul mate" I mean that whenever they were together, they could find something dangerous and exciting to play with. A razor blade discarded in our street. A scorpion in the ruins at Tughlakabad Fort. Together they generated risky fun and they accepted each other completely.

Louis moved back to Canada near the end of third grade. On the weekend after his last day at school, Dave had a goodbye sleepover for him with their friend Sidhu: first swimming at ACSA and then to our house for video games, a chocolate cake by Chote Lal that read "Au Revoir Louis," and a late and rowdy bedtime. Sunday morning was relaxed, with more video games, until the boys' parents picked them up.

On Monday, his first day of school without Louis, Dave was sobbing when he climbed down from the bus and he continued crying as John and I walked him home. I had no sugar coating for him. He'd lost his best friend. That was especially hard in third grade. Second grade had gone well enough, but, except with Louis, he felt like an outsider in third grade. The two other American boys in his class lived on the American compound and had access to their favorite treats, to toys delivered from the States, and to smoothly running American housing. Try as he might, Dave wasn't able to make close friends with them. And one of those boys was a bit of a bully, a macho kid, which was not Dave's style. School felt bleak by the end of third grade.

But as surely as old friends left, new potential friends arrived, and fourth grade was a happy walk in the park for Dave. He and six other little boys were in the same class and on the same Little League team, and they became fast friends. The boys came from the States, Australia, Turkey, India, and England, and they hung out together in and out of school. Dave's fourth-grade journal is full of weekend overnights with pizza and snacks and video games, staying up late together, then swimming together at ACSA the next day. And it helped that they blasted their way through to the New Delhi 1989-1990 Little League Championship. And although the boy who bullied Dave in third grade was in his fourth-grade class, Dave, who did school work easily, sold him homework answers in exchange for American candy. Okay, I know that was wrong, but I said nothing. In fact, I was pleased that Dave was happy with the candy and that to him it was about the candy—just business, nothing personal.

In his fourth-grade journal at the end of the school year, Dave wrote:

"I really liked this class. This has been the best year I've had so far. I wish I could stay another year. I'm sorry I have to leave India this year."

Lynn Litterine

Dave, Louis, and Sidhu at Louis's Goodbye Sleepover

On Assignments with Dad

Marc and Dave took work trips together while we were in India, and Dave had experiences many second-, third-, or fourth-graders didn't have. He and Marc flew to Lumbini, where the Buddha was born and where they shared their hostel room with a huge toad. That night, Dave was allowed to eat just Snickers for supper because their rides to get there in a small plane and a jeep were rough. Once they went to Singapore together, where Dave's first request was for French fries from an airport McDonald's. Marc upgraded them to a deluxe hotel suite and ordered room service, and Dave took a bubble bath. Great start! Later, at the Singapore Zoo, Dave snuggled with an orangutan and its baby. A child could have that kind of experience in non-litigious South Asia. I asked him later what the orangutan felt like, and he said, "prickly and tickley."

Marc Kaufman

David and a New Friend at the Singapore Zoo

After they got back to Delhi, Dave spilled the beans on another one of their Singapore adventures. Entranced by video games at a big department store, Dave ignored Marc's repeated requests to get going, so

Marc walked away for a minute to signal that he was serious. Alone when he looked up, Dave thought Marc really had left, so he left the store and started walking along a busy street nearby. He was a little red-haired boy alone and weeping, not a common sight in Singapore, and a passing driver noticed him, stopped, and offered a ride. Dave got in. It was sheer good luck for us all that the driver was not a predator. Dave remembered the name of the hotel where he was staying, and his rescuer deposited him back at its reception desk. Marc had been frantically calling the clerk, who told Dave, "Your daddy so mad at you." He gave Dave the room key and told him to go up and wait. Marc was overwhelmed by relief, not by anger, when he got back to the hotel. Knowing that divorce—if not homicide—would have followed harm to our son, he told Dave not to tell me what happened, or at least not to tell me right away. To his credit, Dave held out for about two hours before he brought it up. I scolded Marc, "YOU are the grownup. HE is the child." But I also gave Marc a bit of a pass because Singapore was probably the most watched-over city in South Asia, the safest place in which to lose a fourth grader. It levied fines for not flushing public toilets! How did they even know that? Eyes everywhere! If Marc had to lose our son, there was no better place.

In spite of that misadventure, I trusted Marc with Dave's safety when they travelled. The two of them were in Kathmandu when pro-democracy riots broke out against the Nepalese king. Kathmandu was the starting point for a trip Marc planned to Tibet. The Chinese did not allow journalists into Tibet, so Marc's visa said "art historian," and Dave was his camouflage on an innocent father-son trip. Going overland to Lhasa through some of the world's most spectacular scenery would have been adventure enough, but when the riots broke out, Marc had to cover them. Dave was already having fun with friends he met on our earlier trip to Kathmandu. At the Yak and Yeti Hotel, David had met Meepam, an Anglo-Tibetan boy, and his sister, Jade, who were tutored at the hotel. They were there on his second trip, too. So Marc went out to report on the riots, and Dave stayed behind under the supervision of Meepam's mother. Later, Dave wrote for his class newspaper,

> "While my dad was gone we worked out an escape plan. It was to go out the back entrance [of the hotel] and on to one of Mrs. Bolton's friends' houses."

The three kids had fun, some of it at the expense of the Nepali hotel staff, who at one point found the big fountain in the hotel garden foaming with complimentary bubble bath. Dave, Meepam, and Jade watched the riots and troop movements from the hotel roof for a few days, and Marc covered the story down below. Once the daytime curfew was lifted and conditions were safe, Marc took Dave out into the city. By then, explosions were not from artillery fire but from celebratory fireworks; the king had agreed to multi-party government.

* * *

Marc and Dave continued their trip overland to Tibet the day after riots ended in Kathmandu. They crossed high mountain passes in the Himalayas, where a gust of wind could lift Dave, who was sturdy, off his feet. Among flickering lights of butter lamps at monasteries, they saw gold Buddhas encrusted with jewels. At Sera Monastery, Dave met an ancient Mongolian lama who plied him with candy, blessed him by tapping his head with a *sutra* (scroll of Buddhist scripture), and asked him to stay and be a monk.

On Dave's second visit to Sera, a *khampa,* impressed by the lama's interest in Dave, kneeled in front of our 9-year-old son outside the monastery. *Khampas* are known as fierce warriors and skilled horsemen and marksmen. Some have waged guerrilla warfare against the Chinese since the Dalai Lama fled Tibet. The man was imposing, about six feet tall, with long, black hair wound through chunks of coral and turquoise. Because the *khampa* was kneeling, he looked Dave straight in the eye.

"Would the boy give us a blessing?" Passang, Marc's Tibetan guide, translated the *khampa*'s request. She added, "It will please him greatly."

The old lama had blessed Dave with a *sutra,* but all Dave had in his hands was Marc's Canon camera, so he gently touched the top of the man's head with that. The *khampa* stood up and moved away, and the by-then long line of *khampas* that had formed behind him took one step forward. Dave dispensed more blessings, but Marc had reporting to do and finally said, "Let's go." He took Dave's hand and they backed away smiling, nodding, and bowing toward the line. That night by phone from their Lhasa hotel, Dave asked me if he should stay with the old lama and be a monk. He was as serious as any fourth grader could be, but I think the candy was the real attraction. I said, "No."

Thea Patterson, Dave's 4th-grade teacher at AES, excused him from school work for two weeks so that he could go to Tibet. "Your homework is to keep a journal," she said. What does a fourth grader write about Tibet? I still have his notebook.

"... At the beginning it was scary. The roads were unpaved and thin, and we were getting higher and higher. There was rock hanging above us, and a giant gorge below.

Marc Kaufman

Dave and the Mongolian Lama

"... we were in a vast desert, fild with rock, dirt, and wind. ... we came to a tiny house. There we ate a lunch of SPAM eggs and beer. The house was a little house with lamb leg [bones] sticking out of the ceiling.

"... [Xegar Dzong] Each floor of our hotel shared a bathroom, and as if that wasn't enough, going to the bathroom on the ground was cleaner than going in the bathroom provided. I threw up after going into the bathroom.

"... The next morning we went to Tasha Lumpo monestary. There we saw a giant gold bouda made of three tons of pure gold. We also went into a room where they are keeping the tenth Panchin Lama's body. There the monks wanted me to become a monk. The teacher even said I was a lama.

"… [At one village, t]here was way too much food for us so we gave some to the people living there. I watched this one kid who'd go out with a full box and come back a minute later with an empty box.

"… we went to Barkhor. That is a place like a market. The people there all shove things in your face and say, 'Hello! How much!'

"… we went to Potala. That's the Dalai Lama's winter palace. It is huge. Inside there was a tomb made of about 3,721 kg. of pure gold, and turquoise, [garnet], and rubies the size of an adult fist. There's also a statue with 22,000 pearls.

"… In Sera there was an old Mongolian lama who became a lama in one life by memorizing all 100 volumes of the holy scriptures. He was like Santa Claus. …We went to Nenchung monestary. There were really discusting [probably Tantric] paintings on the wall. At Nenchung we learned that all the monks were leaving the monestaries because of Chinese spies.

" … we went to Norbalinca, the Dalai Lama's summer palace. We saw people bow to the 14th Dalai Lama's mother's toilet.

" … The next morning we went back to Drapung. There we found out 200 monks were leaving. We wanted to make sure so we went to Sera [to confirm it]. We found out it was true. We also got a blessing from the Mongolian lama. He blesses you by making you put your head down. He laughs and then hits you on the head with a holy scripter."

From 1987-1990 One Friend Visited

Some of Marc's work colleagues passed through our house on assignments while we lived in India. One of my cousins stopped by for tea, but he was a Pan Am pilot on layover in Delhi, so his was a work trip, too. Our only visit-for-visit's-sake visitors were Marc's parents in 1987 and our supremely loyal friend, Carol, in early 1989. My in-laws had been enthusiastic travelers for years, and their only grandchildren lived in Delhi. Carol would go to the far side of the moon to see her close friends.

I planned a full schedule for her two weeks with us. My friend Deborah suggested a tour of Old and New Delhi with a retired commissary officer she knew through the British High Commission. And I booked a young woman to come and do a *mehndi* (henna) party and invited all my girlfriends and their kids to meet Carol and get hennaed. Marc made sure he'd be home to ride herd on the household during the trip I planned for us to Rajasthan. I even bought tickets to a polo match in Delhi, very Raj. In between, we'd shop and see the New Delhi sights. Two special dinners had to be on the schedule. At home in the States, we caught up with Carol over pizza and ice cream on most Friday nights, so we ordered Nirula's pizza and some of their rose-petal ice cream for one dinner. And Carol was famous back home for her tuna casserole, so I told Chote Lal that she'd want to try his.

Jai Singh and I met her at the airport at the usual time for international arrivals, the middle of the night. I had a marigold *mala* for her, and she looked pretty perky, even after all that flying. Once home, we found it hard to stop talking and go to bed. So many things to talk about—our friends and colleagues at the *Inquirer*, where Carol also worked, and the stories they were covering, their newsroom meltdowns, love affairs, breakups, and divorces; the latest political hijinks in Philadelphia; Carol's 1988 interviews with George H.W. Bush when he was running for president; news about her family in Virginia; and Carol's love life (lately, less than brilliant, she said). But most of all, we retold our favorite stories about each other. Carol brought Marc and I together when we were mooning over each other from separate ends of a newsroom. Her strategy was a dinner party for 12, enough guests that no spotlight would fall on Marc and me. Two years later, she drove from Richmond, VA, to Nyack, NY, through a snowstorm for our wedding reception.

What a comfort it was to make the same old jokes about each other. Our stories were more than words; each was laced through with understandings too specific and mundane to matter to other people. I'd never told those stories to my Delhi friends, so those memories had been silent in me for almost two years before Carol arrived. Together, we three played our accustomed roles in them and finished each other's sentences with the punchlines. For that evening, I was back in the familiar, underscored by Carol's "Oh, y'all!" in her honeyed Virginia accent whenever she was tickled by a memory.

Lynn Litterine

Carol Arrives in Delhi Looking Perky

I wanted to share with Carol the strange adventure that India was for me, and our tour with Nigel, the retired commissary officer, accomplished that. Nigel, Carol, and I piled into the Ford Falcon with Jai Singh behind the wheel. We began tamely enough with a look at Rashtrapati Bhavan; the 340-room home of India's president is at the north end of what was then called Rajpath. Rashtrapati Bhavan had been the home of the British viceroy before Independence. The pink and cream Indian sandstone used to build both it and the India Gate arch at the south end of Rajpath softens the look of the massive structures that were meant to trumpet the power of the Raj.

Nigel then took us to a Hindu cremation ground. We wanted to see places that mattered to Indians, and cremation grounds matter a great deal. But the grounds are also the site of families' grief and should not be treated like a tourist venue. Compared to handing a loved one over to a funeral parlor, Hindu death rites are personal and hands-on. The body is washed, anointed, and clothed in white by family members at home and spends a day there while visitors come and go and Brahmin priests lead rituals. Then the body is carried by men of the family to a cremation ground, where the oldest son of the dead person presides and lights the pyre. We took only two photos. One is of mostly empty pyre sites; the other is of Carol near the huge pile of wood used in the cremations.

The next place we stopped felt ghostly in a way that the cremation ground hadn't. The cremation ground seemed so alive with human ritual and feeling, but in that next place, an arid, sparsely wooded area away from busy parts of the city, monumental statues from the Raj had found their final resting places. Coronation Park was a wasteland, deserted and untended, where the wind stirred up a saltpeter "snow" that had leached out of the ground. Only five of the 19 plinths supported statues moved to the site when British rule ended; the others were empty. The park had been a stage for Raj splendor and power: the venue for ceremony and celebration when Queen Victoria was proclaimed empress of India in 1877, when Edward VII became king of the United Kingdom and emperor of India in 1903, and when George V became emperor of India in 1911. When we visited, it was an outdoor warehouse for five statues, the burial site of an unmourned Raj.

Carol Horner

Delhi Cremation Ground

Carol Horner

Relics of the Raj

When we left the park, Nigel directed Jai Singh to the Delhi city dump because it teemed with lives whose importance to the city Nigel wanted to acknowledge. As instructed, Jai Singh parked the car on the shoulder of an empty road beyond which were acres of land covered in an indistinguishable brown stuff. In the late 1980s, when we stopped by, the refuse of 8,453,000 people was dropped off there; it was already a formidable dump. By 2021, it was nowhere near enough land to deal with the garbage of Delhi's 31,181,376 people, so by then, Delhi had many dumps.

Nigel brought us to the dump to see the heroes of Delhi public sanitation: vultures. At first, we saw nothing but the great expanse of brown; then Nigel took a few firecrackers he'd brought with him and walked out onto the trash. He lit one, and at its *kapow*, hundreds and hundreds of vultures took to the air. They were big birds, and the sound of their wings made a remarkable *whoosh*. The vultures congregated at the dump, but their food runs crisscrossed the whole city, where they were a crucial barrier to the spread of disease. Large animals, including cattle and pigs, roamed the streets of Delhi and sometimes died on them, and their bodies were left to rot. But vultures eat carrion, and their remarkable digestive tracts neutralize the pathogens in it. The threat of human illness ends in the vultures' guts.

Unfortunately, in the 1990s, a few years after our visit to the dump, the vulture population collapsed by 95 per cent across India. Instead, feral dogs ate street carrion and increased in number with an accompanying increase in rabies, anthrax, and plague. The crow population also prospered without the vultures and spread pathogens to poultry and to humans. The cause of the collapse in the vulture population was finally identified; diclofenac, an anti-inflammatory given to livestock, was fatal to vultures. The drug was banned in 2006, but vulture populations have not yet recovered. The estimate of 40 million vultures in India in the 1980s had dropped to 19,000 by 2017 (News 18).

I'm glad we saw them at the height of their power and wellbeing.

Lynn Litterine

Carol at a Spice Merchant's Shop in Old Delhi

Our last stop with Nigel was the markets of Old Delhi, which was a lot like stepping into the Bible. Narrow, twisting alleys were lined with open stalls that sold mounded spices, metal pots, boiled milk, and bread. The pathways were jammed with people and animals, and I tamped down panic as I shifted from side to side to thread my way through them trying not to think about what would happen if a bullock startled and ran.

Carol Horner

A Bullock on a Packed Street in Old Delhi

Nigel led us through the crowds to his objective, a low doorway on a tiny side alley. We ducked through it into a dark room. At first, I saw nothing, but I smelled cattle dung and heard low huffing noises. When my eyes adjusted, I saw that we shared a small room with a bullock.

"What you see here has not changed for thousands of years," Nigel said. "This is a working oil press exactly like the ancient ones."

A worn post as fat as a tree trunk was in the middle of the room, and the bullock was hitched to it by an equally worn wood and iron neckpiece. The animal plodded in a circle, the post turned a wheel below it, and the wheel ground oil out of seeds. Although the bullock looked underfed, someone had taken the trouble to color its horns light blue. I had no problem believing Nigel: I was looking back 2,000 years in time.

* * *

"Who's the bride?" Meera translated for the young woman who'd come to do our *mehndi* party. My friends, women in their 40s with children, laughed. Weddings were a long time ago for all of us, but the young woman's question was appropriate. A women-only *mehndi* party usually precedes an Indian wedding, part of glamming up for the main event. A *mehndi* artist draws designs on guests' hands and feet with a paste of powdered henna leaves and water. The paste dries and, when rinsed off, leaves the designs dyed into the skin. The henna designs look like lace and last for a week or two. When I arrived in India, they put me off; the reddish-brown lines looked like Mercurochromed sutures, not like glamorous makeup. But I'd gotten used to them, liked them even, and knew *mehndi* had to be part of Carol's visit.

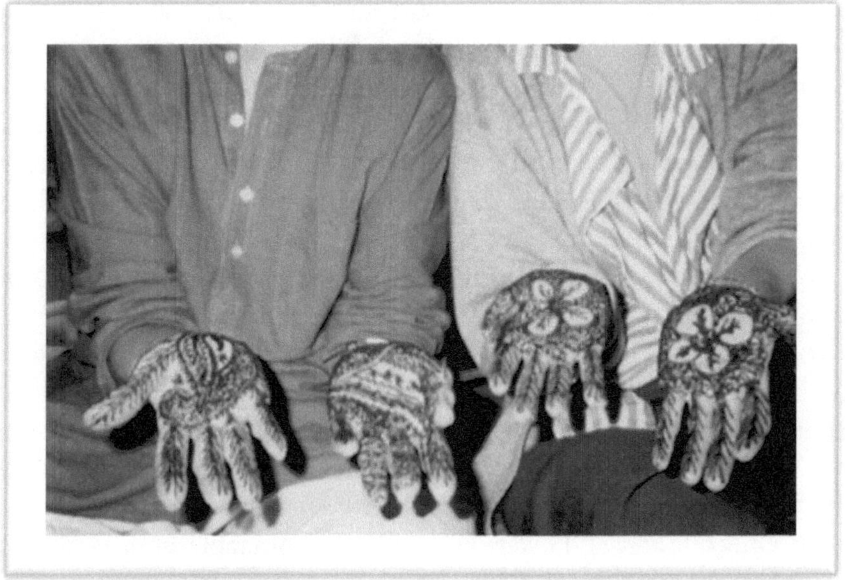

Marc Kaufman

A Stylized Mango on My Right Hand and Flowers for Carol

The girl who drew the designs we each requested was chaperoned by her elderly grandfather, so she was young, but her work was as good as a grown woman's. Days later, on our visit to a village in Rajasthan, local women gathered around us to inspect our hands. Murmurs of approval followed as they flipped our hands from palm to back to palm again. "Very pretty, very pretty," our host translated for us.

* * *

That host was a Rajasthani *thakur*, a hereditary nobleman, and the village was in the desert outside Jodhpur. Carol and I were the only guests at *Rohet Garh*, the *thakur*'s ancestral home, built in the 16th century. The compound was surrounded by a high stone wall interrupted only by a wooden gate so high, we could have ridden through on horseback instead of in our taxi. The inner courtyard was sunny, covered in well-tended grass, and dotted with trees and lawn chairs. Songbirds called and a flock of little parrots flew from tree to tree. Peacocks strutted on the lawn. The estate included 384 villages in the surrounding desert and was given to the *thakur*'s family after a military victory four centuries earlier. Our host, Manvendra Singh, governed the surrounding villages differently than his noble forebears did. He was their political representative in Parliament. But the land was still his, and when we traveled over it with him, villagers treated him like the 12th generation feudal lord he was. He seemed to have their affection, too.

We had first taken a train from Delhi to the city of Jodhpur in the Thar Desert. We had lunch in the garden at *Umaid Bhawan*, a hotel in the palace of Jodhpur's former maharaja. Even at that 5-star hotel, we were cautious at lunch: a grilled cheese sandwich for me and a grilled cheese sandwich with tomato for Carol. Alas, that tomato. We continued out into the desert to *Rohet Garh* by taxi, and by suppertime, Carol was retching into a basin in our darkened room and waved me off to eat alone with Mr. Singh. Only our host and I were at the dining room table, and, as we tried to ignore the sounds of Carol being sick that—unbelievably—came through even the thick stone walls, he asked me questions about our lives in the States. He had lived in San Francisco for a while as the Indian consul and was a kind, cultured, educated man, in no way provincial. The description of my life, a married mother caring for two boys while her husband worked, glided easily past him, but he looked puzzled when I described Carol's life. Married and divorced early, she was a full-time journalist who owned her own home and made her own way through life as it suited her.

"Her life is not possible here," he said. He meant neither approval nor disapproval; he was simply stating the fact of the chasm between Philadelphia and rural Rajasthan in 1989. Progress for women was happening in India, but it wasn't because Indira Gandhi had been in power. As tough as she was, her power was inherited from her father via electoral politics. But in Delhi in 1989, Kiran Bedi was making waves as a police official, and *Manushi: A Journal about Women and Society*, had been unabashedly feminist and activist since 1978. Farther afield, women in villages were setting up their own cooperatives for small business loans. But a cultural chasm still yawned, even between Indian and western feminists. Like when a young woman who worked as an editor at *Manushi* said to an American friend of mine, "You mean your families leave you to go alone to bars to meet men?" She was not impressed by our way of doing things *and* she was a feminist.

In conversational pauses, Mr. Singh and I still heard Carol retching, and, in between questions   and answers, he pressed me to let him call the "compounder" to treat her. His description made clear that the compounder wasn't a doctor or even a pharmacist; he was "like a pharmacist" ... sort of. But Mr. Singh voiced the utmost faith in him and was clearly upset that a guest was sick. He finally convinced me, and when I returned to our room after supper, Carol had had enough, too.

"Call the compounder," she said.

The man who arrived with Mr. Singh in the darkness outside the door to our room was not wearing a white coat, not a long one or even a short one. In fact, he was dressed like he'd just finished a shift on a garbage truck. He was wearing worn and stained clothes, a navy-blue watch cap, and old leather sandals. Mr. Singh translated: the compounder would give Carol a shot. The shot was given. We paid the compounder a miniscule amount, and he left. Within a half hour, Carol was deeply asleep, and in the morning, she was restored. In our subsequent travels around Mr. Singh's land, village elders offered us opium as routine hospitality. Since neither of us was interested, Mr. Singh coached us on how to decline politely, which we did. However, if I were to guess, I'd say that at least once in her life, my well-behaved friend had opium.

*Carol **Horner***

Opium Hospitality** Offered to Us by a Village **Elder

With Carol fully recuperated, we toured with Mr. Singh. He took us to his family's tiny temple on a hill overlooking the desert, to the huts of artisans and sellers of modestly priced antiques, and on a nighttime camel ride across the desert. The desert under moonlight was beautiful, but, like in Delhi, the camel's breath was rank and I fought off motion sickness from all the rolling.

Rajput nobles like Mr. Singh's forebears were warriors, and in any defeat, their women would be raped and enslaved by the victors. Only death could keep the women from that, and prominent on the Singh compound wall next to the big gate were handprints of women in the family who had performed *suttee,* the immolation of widows. Perhaps a proud noblewoman raised in Rajput culture would willingly throw herself on a pyre to avoid rape and enslavement; perhaps some women were "encouraged" to do so. The culture gap and the centuries between me and those Rajputs distorted any understanding I could reach about *suttee.* In

Delhi, newspapers still carried occasional stories of young women "encouraged" to self-immolate by in-laws who wanted more dowry and didn't get it. Every culture has its crazy reasons for hurting women, and it's not a welcome topic for conversation. I didn't feel comfortable enough to ask Mr. Singh about the handprints next to the gate until the end of our visit. By then, the powder on the handprints had been refreshed, which gave me an opening to ask about them. In his answer, I heard a cultured, kind host who accepted the past enough to keep the women's handprints fresh. I believe he did so to honor the women, but I liked our host and didn't want to ask him if I was right.

Carol Horner

Jauhar (Self-Immolation) Handprints Next to the Compound Gate

* * *

Back in Delhi again, our time together was almost over. We had left only the polo match I'd bought tickets for, and it was a first for both of us. The venue was modest: a grassy field, a wooden field house and bleachers, and traffic noise from the Delhi streets outside the grounds. Polo is a terrifying game to watch. Horses gallop full tilt towards each other as their riders lean far out of their saddles to swing wood mallets that send a ball traveling at around 110 mph. The 4-ounce ball of wicker or bamboo is hard; my guess was that it could shatter a kneecap, which might be preferable to colliding with a 1,000-pound horse at full gallop or getting beaned by a mallet. I left the game impressed by the skill, courage, and insanity of the players.

Our final supper together was, of course, Chote Lal's tuna casserole. Random fate smiled on his work, and only tuna meat was in the can, not roe. Carol gave the casserole two thumbs up and said it would be a knockout at any Virginia church supper. Because our family didn't get sick afterward, I don't think the casserole was responsible for what happened to Carol on the long flight home. I think she had a taste of something ill-advised at the airport or on the plane—she thought maybe it was yogurt—and she wound up locked in the plane's bathroom retching yet again until a cabin attendant ordered her out for the landing in Philadelphia. With no compounder on call, she left the plane in a wheelchair.

Letter Home to an Old Friend
Two Years and Four Months In

Oct. 25, 1989

Dear Diane,

My last 7 months in India now—I thought the last year would be the easiest, but I'm a nervous wreck. All the culture shock (this place can be horrifying to the likes of us), single parenting, and aloneness has gotten to me—coping with some anxiety attacks and (unheard of in me) insomnia. I feel I'm finally beginning to let sink in what I've been feeling for 3 years ... I don't regret it, and I won't leave early, but the emotional price is high. Kids, at least, are flourishing—great year at school for both. Rajiv Gandhi has considerately called for elections, so Marc's on 2- or 3-day trips in India, instead of 1-month trips under fire in Afghanistan— our family appreciates the respite ... I'm shopping for ... final treasures, and getting as much tailoring done as I can. It's finally down to the 80s daytime, so cool season has arrived ... Love, Lynn

Meltdowns Nos. 3 and 4: The Big Ones

I have always felt porous to what's happening around me; I may get confused about where I end and the rest of the world starts. When I heard bad news in Delhi, I saw targets on the kids' backs and mine. Bad news could get very bad, like the fulminant hepatitis A that killed an American aid worker who politely drank unboiled village water. Good manners could kill you in India. What if? What if?

What if one of the boys was cut beyond what I could fix with my butterfly bandages? What if diarrhea got beyond my control in one of their small bodies? What if a fever got dangerously high? For the best treatment, you did not go to an Indian hospital back then. In a news story that ran for days in Delhi, an operating room at a big hospital could not be brought back to sterile condition. Personnel were mystified until they discovered a hole to the outside behind an operating room wall and the mother cat who had nested between the outer and inner walls to deliver her litter. I collected names of the small, private clinics friends used and recommended. What if? What if?

Transfusions were out of the question; India didn't test its blood supply for AIDS, but AIDS was there. Officials variously ignored the problem or downplayed it or said it occurred only among African immigrants. Some foreigners started a grassroots blood-type registry and pledged ourselves free of AIDS and willing to donate blood. If someone among our families needed a transfusion, they would take their chances on malaria but not on AIDS. What if? What if?

My own emergencies were minor, but they unsettled me. Once, as I waited outside John's nursery classroom at AES, a beehive the size of a watermelon emptied into the schoolyard packed with 4-year-olds. The swarm attacked kids, teachers, and waiting moms. We rushed children inside and treated the stings. We were lucky that the afternoon class had no kids or teachers with bee allergies. What if? What if?

Eventually my limited coping "strategy" —trying to plan for all eventualities, squaring my shoulders, and marching on—was bound to fail. The what-ifs overwhelmed me one night about two and a half years into our stay. Marc was out of town, and I went out that evening to a dinner party while Meera babysat the boys. When I came home, I felt a little nauseous. Although it might have been a germ, what was more likely was that the stress chemicals chronically pumping through my body made me feel sick. My inadequate coping strategy collapsed. "Hepatitis!" I panicked, and more stress chemicals poured into my bloodstream. When I began to shake, my nerves went wild.

It was late, but I called Lisa, my friend down the street, and, within minutes, she and her husband, Tom, showed up at the door radiating calm. They drove me to East West Clinic, which was run by an Indian doctor many of us knew and trusted. "Have you been vomiting?" a series of nurses asked me over and over. I said "no" each time, sure that it was only a matter of minutes before I would. IV hydration was the first go-to treatment for most illnesses in India, so, vomiting or not, they hooked me up to a line. Lisa stayed to eyeball the IV bags and make sure the solution was clear; quality control could be an issue with more than canned tuna or face cream. She stretched out to rest on a cot in the room but got up to inspect each new bag. I made frequent trips to the bathroom to pee. Hours passed with lots of peeing but no vomiting. Somewhere among those many trips to the bathroom, I realized that my problem was anxiety, not hepatitis. I wasn't sick; I was afraid of getting sick. In fact, I'd been afraid of that since we arrived in India. I told Lisa, we told the nurses, and the IV port was removed. Lisa went home, and, in a few hours, Marc returned from wherever he'd been on assignment and collected me from the clinic.

Here's what the Mayo Clinic says about chronic stress:

> "The body's stress response system is usually self-limiting. Once a perceived threat has passed, hormone levels return to normal. ... But when stressors are always present and you constantly feel under attack, that fight-or-flight reaction stays turned on.
>
> "The long-term activation of the stress response system and the overexposure to cortisol and other stress hormones that follows ... puts you at increased risk of ...

Anxiety
Depression
Digestive problems
Sleep problems"

What-ifs never end; they keep opening out into the future, so my cortisol and adrenaline levels were chronically primed. For a while after the clinic visit, I steadied myself in spite of them, but eventually, when Marc was away on another assignment, I ran offtrack again. That day, too, I was fine until bedtime. I settled the boys for the night then took a shower. I read for a while in bed, and, when I started drifting off mid-sentence, I turned off the light. I was nearly asleep when a grotesque face flew up into my head from someplace primal, and I woke with a jerk and a pounding heart. The face disappeared as soon as I was fully awake, and I gradually relaxed and began to drift off again. But a different demon face flew up, and that happened again and again. And then again and again the next night. I was exhausted but couldn't sleep because of the awful faces that suddenly showed up whenever I nodded off. I'd spent two nights with only bits and pieces of sleep when Deborah called to chat, and I told her what was happening. Her husband worked for the British government, so they had medical care.

"I'll stop at the High Commission for some meds and be right over," she said.

She arrived at my house with a bottle of beta blockers. Not strictly proper for the English doctor to dispense to me, of course, but this was India and spouses traveled and friends helped friends. "These may help for now," she said. I took some, and either the pills or Deborah's steady presence next to me on the couch worked. I fell asleep, and she sat nearby for my whole nap. No monsters.

When I told a friend what happened, she put me in touch with the psychiatrist at the American Embassy. Like the English doctor, Fred was a practitioner I had no right to treatment from. Amazing to me since he was responsible for American government employees in Pakistan and Bangladesh in addition to India, he made time for us to talk. I didn't see him weekly, but I saw him often enough to calm down, and he made sure I had one Xanax for bedtime every night. The horrible faces never returned.

On one visit, Fred told me, "Jung described India as 'the mind turned inside out,'" And that's what it felt like my mind had done; its primal soup had risen to the top. After Fred said that, I had permission to see that what I was doing in India was hard because he saw it as hard.

When, a few weeks later, Marc asked, "Do you want to go home?" I could genuinely say, "No, I want to stay."

Thailand

Instead of moving back home, we went to the most un-Indian place we could think of: Phuket, Thailand. To travel from India to Thailand is to move from a strict, arbitrary social order to one based on *sanuk*, a Thai word that means "having fun." *Sanuk* isn't just an option in life; it's a goal.

> "The Thais have elevated fun to an ethos, a way of life … *Sanuk* is not fun as mindless diversion or frivolity; it's fun as an intrinsically valuable activity." (BBC)

I can illustrate the feeling of *sanuk* with our hotel lobby, which was open on all sides to a light breeze from the Andaman Sea and smelled of the tropical flowers in vases on every tabletop. Or by the massage I had on the warm sand of the hotel's beach. Or by the twisting water slides I rode with the boys into hotel swimming pools. Or by the patio chess set that was taller than David. But for me, the Thai guys running a parasailing business nearby were super-*sanuk*. Their eyes were bloodshot, and I could smell marijuana smoke around their small shed, but I didn't care. I was determined to prove to myself that, in spite of meltdowns, I could still have fun, especially "as an intrinsically valuable activity." The young men laid out a multi-colored parachute on the beach behind me and hitched me to it with a harness. Then they hitched the parachute line to a sleek motorboat, climbed into the boat, and gunned it.

Suddenly I wasn't standing on the beach; I was hanging in the sky over blue water dotted with jellyfish the size of cake plates. Except for me and my parachute, the sky was empty. Uncontrollable laughter and whooping bubbled up out of me. I had all the space I needed and three stoned beach boys to guide my flight. It was total *sanuk* and it was definitely intrinsically valuable to me. I remembered some of the best parts of who I was. Photos Marc took show me as a dot the size of a mosquito hanging from the parachute. I laughed and whooped until the boat slowed and I floated gently down into the warm sea.

Marc Kaufman

All the Space I Needed

For three or four days, we ate breakfast near the pool, we played chess on the giant chessboard, we slid down the water slides, and Marc and I ate dinner alone each night at the hotel's open-air restaurant while Dave and John played at the kids' center. After we picked them up, we'd go to the beach and watch luminescent jellyfish light up when we stirred the water with our feet. By the time we arrived in Bangkok for New Year's Eve, we were loudly singing carols in the taxi from the airport.

A Lump in the Road

Then, shortly after we returned from Bangkok, a big what-if showed up. I found a lump in my breast. One of my friends was the wife of an embassy doctor. That's how I found myself one evening on their bed at home while Hope held my hand and her husband tried to aspirate the lump. When nothing came up in the syringe, David said, "It's not a cyst. You have to go to Bangkok or Singapore and have it removed and tested. The testing here isn't up to it, too many power fluctuations."

I wanted Marc with me if I needed surgery, so he came home from whatever assignment he was on, and, for the first time in India, we both left the boys behind. David went to stay with Lisa, Tom, their kids, and the miniature railroad. John went with Meera to stay with the family from *The Washington Post;* the mom there was also a friend of mine.

The night before we went to see our Thai surgeon, Marc and I went to Bangkok's charm market, a bustling place after dark. Gold charms were for sale for hundreds, maybe thousands, of dollars, and "white metal" charms were for sale for chump change. They all seemed to cover the same issues—business success, health, love, deflection of evil intentions. I didn't know whether the level of protection rose with the price, but I couldn't afford the gold ones anyway, so I bought a "good-health Buddha" with pocket money. What I remember about the market late that night is the feel of it—the noise of many voices calling out, the light from hundreds of bare bulbs strung over the alleyways between booths, the crowd milling about, and the cozy smell of wood smoke from barbecue stands. It was a bubbling human scene that made me feel less alone about what the next day might bring.

The following morning at Samitivej Hospital, in an exam room like one in any American hospital, a surgeon palpated the lump in my breast and decided that it had to come out. "Round and smooth, probably not a problem, but I don't leave it in a woman your age," by which I think he meant "young-ish." Later, on the operating table, I told him, "I bought a charm for this last night." "Must have been expensive," he said. "No, it was cheap," I told him and suddenly wished I'd sprung for 24-carat gold instead of "white metal."

Medical care in Bangkok mixed up-to-date technology and hygiene with warm personal service. The whole time I was on the operating table awake under a local anesthetic, a nurse held my hand, another nurse assisted the surgeon, and yet another nurse translated into approximate English anything the surgeon said. The lump was dispatched to the lab, and we waited in the operating room for preliminary results. Soon a technician returned and announced something in Thai that made all three nurses happy. "Lipoma! Lipoma!" they cheered. "Fat tumor!" my translator announced. If I'd been dressed, I'd have taken a victory lap of the OR to their applause. The surgeon stitched me up, and Marc and I went home to Delhi, to our kids, and to our friends. Some weeks later, a letter came from the hospital reporting the conclusive biopsy results: I was in the clear. More than 30 years later, my "good-health Buddha" hangs from our car's rearview mirror. It's not a "no-accidents Buddha," but I'm sticking with it anyway.

Letter Home to an Old Friend Two Years and Eight Months In

Feb. 3, 1990

Dear Diane,

We're down to our last 4 months, thank goodness—I'm really burnt out this year, too much Third World, too much single parenting, too much apart from Marc. Insomnia and anxiety attacks hit last fall. I've talked and grown my way out of some of it plus a little medication from the embassy shrink, but a change in our lives is the final cure. We decided we needed a break, so the four of us went to a resort in southern Thailand for Christmas. It was great. Massages on the beach, jet skiing with the kids, I went parasailing just to prove I could—we ate lots of fresh seafood, terrific little pineapples, and good Singha beer (the beer here has had muck in it lately). It allowed me to recall that life can be pretty and fun, <u>and</u> that I have a good marriage ... It's still cool enough in Delhi for me to comfortably race-walk, but the temp spikes next month, 90s in April, 100s in May ... We're both doing our farewell shopping—Marc bought 8 or 10 rugs on his last trip to Kabul (lowest prices in S. Asia); I keep getting one "last" pair of silk pants tailored (for $7 or $10!) or buying one more hand-beaded or hand-embroidered shawl; fancy placemats here cost 50 cents each (I keep seeing Bloomie's prices superimposed on them like a bad dream). ... Love, Lynn

Destructive Goodbyes

I can't say with certainty why this particular scenario kept playing out in Delhi: often, when only a few weeks were left before a foreign family headed home for good, someone among their previously rock-solid household staff would veer wildly offtrack. They would get drunk on duty or suddenly stop showing up or start fighting bitterly with the people they had happily worked with up to that moment.

At our house, it was Jai Singh who veered. We came home from dinner with friends to find Meera in tears. While she was babysitting the boys, Jai Singh had stopped by. Whatever disagreement occurred between them, he had slapped her and left. Jai Singh, Meera, and Chote Lal formed my three-headed god of household stability. Some flirtatiousness existed between Jai Singh and Meera, but Chote Lal always kept an eye on that and chided Meera when he thought it went too far. Because Meera gave Chote Lal the deference she would to her own father, life in our house had trotted along peacefully.

But Meera was an independent spirit, too independent for her gender and class in India. She told me that neighbors would watch and comment on her comings and goings, especially when she was dropped off at home in the dark by Jai Singh after babysitting. And during my lumpectomy in Thailand, when she and John stayed with our friends, their *ayah* spoke disapprovingly to them about Meera's friendship with Jai Singh. But we were in no position to weigh those complaints because even a friendship between an Indian woman and a man could stir up talk in Delhi.

We'd long before accepted that we'd never completely understand what went on among the people who worked for us. We'd learned that early via the anonymous letter about Margaret stealing. We might work out some of the Indian context for things that happened in our house but never more than some. And, since the power ratio between us and the people who worked for us was unbalanced, we had no right to their complete honesty.

So, we acted on the facts we knew: we'd soon be leaving, and Marc could drive our car around Delhi in the meantime; the boys were close to Meera, and she was an important part of their lives all day long; Jai Singh had slapped her and didn't deny that. We had no way of knowing if he'd do it again, and we absolutely did not want any rough stuff in our house. So, Marc fired Jai Singh, who did not protest. Marc wrote him a strong recommendation as a driver and translator because Jai Singh deserved one; he was excellent at his job.

The thoughts I have now are about the part we might have played in what happened. I consider how it must have felt for servants to routinely learn the ways of new families and then say good-bye over and over again to those employers whose lives they'd shared. Our household's warmth toward us, especially toward the boys, was genuine, but we'd never be a part of their lives that they could count on long term. Like many of our foreign friends, we were good employers, and that may have made our departure harder. Was getting fired a faster, neater break for Jai Singh? Or maybe he already had another job he had to start?

I also wonder whether we did both Meera and Jai Singh a disservice. Our American ideas about the individual were the polar opposite of how the two of them lived in their communities. As a man, Jai Singh had greater freedom than Meera did, not absolute freedom but greater than hers. Like many young Indian men, Jai Singh had worked abroad in Dubai and sent money back to his family, but when he worked for us, he lived with his father, mother, wife, and children in Delhi. Indian family practices dictated that his father headed the family. How did that sit with a young man who'd lived overseas? How did he feel being in his 30s and subservient to his father? We had benefited from the cosmopolitanism he'd developed abroad. He was bright, his English was perfect to the point of punning, he understood our questions about Indian life in the broadest sense, and he was comfortable with us. He spent his workdays in America and went home to traditional India.

We encouraged Meera's independence, too. She was as bright as Jai Singh and equally fluent in English. She understood the child-rearing practices I asked her to use: following the boys' interests in activities and not imposing her adult agenda, setting limits on poor behavior, not running to them right away when they fell, reading to them when they asked instead of doing her chores. But unlike a Bollywood starlet, Meera didn't have the money and power to back up independent behavior. And her own family was fractured, a fact whose significance I see only in hindsight. For reasons I never learned, her father lived full time back in his home village. Her two brothers lived at their jobs in Delhi. So, Meera's mother nominally headed their nearly all-female household, and that was not traditional. One older sister had married and moved out. Another older sister seemed to be fragile in some way and wasn't married or asked to go out to work. The son and daughter of an older brother also lived with them. That nephew in his early teens was the only male in their house. While we were there, both Meera's brother-in-law and the brother who was the father of her niece and nephew died. In traditional Indian terms, theirs was a ship without a captain on deck.

While in India, I read the work of the Indian psychotherapist, author, and academic, Sudhir Kakar. Kakar trained with Erik Erikson and at the Sigmund Freud Institute in Germany, so he had a foot planted firmly in India and a foot planted firmly in the west. In *The Inner World: A Psychoanalytic Study of Childhood and Society in India*, he explains his understanding of the workings of traditional India: to be "good" is to conform to family and community mores. Until a child is about four years old, he writes, the mother interprets and insists on what is "good"; after that, male relatives and the larger community do that shaping of character. Conscience is located outside the individual in what Kakar calls "external 'watchmen'" (p. 135), and those watchmen have a responsibility to enforce community mores. The system is stable, but "[d]ifficulties arise when the pace of change quickens," Kakar writes (p. 108).

For Jai Singh, that pace must have quickened the moment he set out on his independent life in Dubai. For Meera, it quickened when her nearly all-female household left its village for the big city and needed the income that Meera's work life provided. Jai Singh returned from Dubai to a traditional life. But independent Meera had enjoyed our family's ways of doing things, and she made a more radical choice when we were packing up to leave. She took a job with an American diplomat who was returning to the States and could legally bring her in with his family. Had Jai Singh's slap been a reaction to Meera's plan, whatever their relationship had been—friends, flirts, or lovers? Kakar writes that when community authority over an individual lessens because of social changes, "a volatile aggressiveness ... can quickly flare ..." (p. 136). I'll never know what happened that night between Jai Singh and Meera, but Kakar's book made sense of much that I saw in India, at least in the city: waves of change coursing through communities and destabilizing traditional social controls. As for me, I was done with my India adventure and ready to go home.

Departure—June 1990

We were excited to be headed back to a familiar and easier life in Pennsylvania, but the practical aspects of leaving Delhi had to be faced first. We hired a local company to sell off for a commission most of our household goods. The sale took place inside our house, and the company hired guards to admit two or three people at a time from the crowd waiting outside and to keep an eye on them as they shopped. Untaxed foreign goods were tempting.

Another company packed up what we were taking home, but first, the representative had a question: Did we want chemicals or peppercorns in the shipment to keep out pests? A few foreigners who represented chemical companies had told me how careless Indian handling of chemicals was—enabled and encouraged by those same foreigners playing down the dangers of what they were selling. So, I definitely wanted peppercorns, and peppercorns I was given. To this day, one usually rolls across the floor when I go digging among Marc's stored rugs.

Once the house was empty, we spent our last Delhi evening at a friend's home in our neighborhood. Wise by then in the uncertain ways of travel in South Asia, Marc called the airline to check on our flight out: CANCELLED WITHOUT NOTICE. India was not going to let go of us easily.

"Get some sleep with the kids," he said. "I'll go out to the airport and be an angry foreigner." Marc isn't easily angered, but it was still his practice not to offer *baksheesh*, so he would need to argue our way onto a flight.

Our friends' guest bedroom was hot, but the boys were already sound asleep in a shared bed. Earlier, they'd exchanged hugs with the people in our household. They hadn't cried over the good-byes; by then, they were looking forward to a vacation in Japan and Hawaii on our way home. I was still wide awake in the heat. Our household staff had dissolved into jobs with other families. Our home had been emptied. Our car had been sold. Our belongings had been shipped. We had no place in India, and I wanted to go home.

Eventually Marc slipped back into the guest room and whispered, "We're set. I got another flight." We packed up, woke the kids, and, without having slept ourselves, headed to the airport.

Since he was a newborn, awake and trying to see the hospital nursery around him, Dave has always liked to know exactly what's up, so the mysterious margarine and Nestle's Quik deliveries to our kitchen had piqued his curiosity for several years; he often questioned me hard about who brought the contraband from the commissary. I held onto the secret but promised to tell him when the landing gear lifted on our final flight home. Dave also never forgets a promise. As soon as the wheels finished creaking into their bays, he asked, "Who brought the margarine and Nestle's Quik?"

"Lisa," I said.

"I knew it!" he crowed.

And that's how we left India.

Busted on the Big Island

When Marc and I were in Bangkok to have that breast lump removed, I'd stocked up on my bedtime helper, Xanax, for the last few months in Delhi. In Thailand, it was sold legally without a prescription and was dispensed in empty film cans. On the flight from Japan to Hawaii, I did something Marc warns against: I told the truth on my customs form. I had three years' worth of Indian jewelry in my suitcase that I had not wanted to trust to the household shipment. The jewelry wasn't 22-karat gold, but it was nice enough silver that I pegged it all at about $400 on the form. That amount triggered an inspection of my suitcase. And that was how I got busted in Honolulu in front of my kids.

I'd lived in South Asia long enough that it didn't occur to me that a film can of Xanax pills with no prescription would be a problem. When the customs agent, alerted by my $400 jewelry estimate, decided to look through my suitcase, she found the film can of prescriptionless Xanax and pulled us out of line for a more rigorous inspection of my bags. The boys were wide-eyed. The agent found nothing else illegal, confiscated the Xanax, and let me go. I wasn't looking forward to bedtime that night without a pill, but, as we left the airport, Marc, my hero, said, "Don't worry, Lynnie. I have one tablet in my pocket." On sunny, warm Hawaii in the company of old friends who met us there, that one pill was enough. No scary faces showed up subsequently when I fell asleep, and that marked the end of my Xanax phase. Welcome home, adventurer.

Accepting Contradictions

My reactions to India often squared off against each other, and I struggled to reconcile those ill-tempered pairings into Perfect Adventure Mind. But perfection, I realize now, were it even possible, is static and leads nowhere. A therapist once asked me what doing things perfectly would feel like. "A hum," I said. "Lynn," that wise woman told me, "when you hear the hum, you know you're dead."

I've worked to accept my version of India, no one else's, and to not punish myself for what that version was or was not. It included both the excitement of adventure and the nagging of what-ifs. The adventurer in me believed that a life well-lived meant meeting challenges in interesting places. The worrier in me was committed to heading off what-ifs and was scared of what failure to do that might bring. But some failure is inevitable anywhere, and I wasn't just anywhere. I was on an adventure in a strange and confusing place, and I was often on my own and responsible for my children.

Both the adventurer and the worrier were me. Both had plusses; the adventurer made me grow, and the worrier prepared for problems that I could actually head off. Both had minuses; the adventurer sometimes exposed me to scarier risks than I wanted to handle, and the worrier overwhelmed me with concerns I couldn't address. One thing was certain after India: neither of them was going to give up and go away. But India gave me practice in holding contradictions: the sacred as seductive Krishna and the maternal as fanged Kali; the fragrance of night-blooming jasmine over the gauntlet of pig poop in the street; the gold-embroidered *sarees* and the beggars' filthy rags; the raw power of caste and the practice of nonviolence; the poor, itinerant laborer and his sublime song to the rain. I had to open my mind wide enough to take all that in and hold it. Reality was complex. India was complex. I was complex. Like an entwined god and goddess, I had to be both my opposites to be complete. It would have been unwise—it would have been impossible—it still is—to choose between them. Where opposites meet, new ideas fly off like sparks. That was India's biggest, best, and most challenging lesson for me, and because of it, I cherish the time I spent there.

Bonus Lessons

Adventures or Vacations?

Adventures and what-ifs go hand in hand. An adventure is never a vacation. An adventure is for growing into the challenges you meet along the way, and you need to do some planning and some suffering for that. A vacation is for relaxing into yourself. Both have their uses, but be clear about which you're setting out on.

Predictability or Flexibility?

Predictability cannot increase flexibility because predictability contains no surprises to which you must react.

Stark Contrasts

Stark contrasts are unsettling, but they stimulate thoughts and feelings and cannot be found in American suburbs.

"First" and "Third" Worlds

The phrases "first world" and "third world" apply to economies and material wealth, not to intellectual sophistication or spiritual riches.

Life and Death and Life and Death and Life and ... etc.

From a Hindu perspective, worlds bubble up over and over in the cosmic ocean, and each bubble plays out four epochs. Our world is in the epoch of *Kali Yuga,* which might last 432,000 years or 1,080,000 years, depending on whom you consult. Ours is the age of the demon Kali (not the goddess Kali), a time of darkness, sin, misery, conflict, and lies. We have a long way to go to get out of it; *Kali Yuga* is said to have begun in 3102 BCE. But don't lose heart; take the long view: Kali Yuga will die and our world's next rebirth brings *Satya Yuga,* an age of truth and intrinsic goodness. Whether in worlds or in people, life and death must both occur for either to occur because life and death are entwined like a god and his *shakti.* In the United States, life is mostly what meets our eyes; death is nearly invisible. Invisibility gives death an uncanniness that unsettles us. And death's invisibility feeds a false hope that mishap, sickness, maybe even death itself, can be avoided if we just try hard enough to do everything as we should—healthy food, exercise, checkups and vaccinations, self-care to relieve stress. That's the outlook of a young and unsophisticated culture.

Life Stages

What happened around me in India gave me joy and appalled me but was always rich and made me think more and feel more. Decades later, I look at the influence of my life in Delhi on my life now and hope that the meaning I derive from it is honest, respectful, and interesting because India can withstand honesty and is worthy of respect and interest. These final sections are not how I would have described my reactions in 1990 when I came home. These thoughts were not available to me then. I was 44 years old, running a household, caring for two boys, and, beginning in 1991, earning bachelor's and master's degrees. Now I'm 79, my little boys are grown men, and one is a father himself. I watch him and his wife with my grandson and marvel at how much work they do. I no longer know myself as the person who did that much in a day. Life reshapes me, and the world looks different from each new shape I take.

Ashramas are the traditional four life stages described by Hinduism: student, householder, forest dweller, and wandering ascetic. I'm at *vanaprastha*, forest dweller, a partial retirement from the world. I've left busy-busy *gṛhastha*, a stage of working, of raising children, and of running a home. Big job that! I'm glad I did it, and I'm glad it's done. *Vanaprastha* is spacious and peaceful, more like cow-dust hour. In *vanaprastha*, I want to remember with gratitude the joys I've had, and I want to summon the courage I need to go eventually into the greatest unknown. The joy is easy, and I've received more of it than I dared hoped. The courage is difficult because fear is its implied companion; without fear, I wouldn't need courage. Living constructively and graciously with the loss of people I loved, with diminishing physical ability, and with my own looming mortality is hard. I'm lonely for those people; I miss my oh-so-capable body; and, yes, I'm scared by death. I know that sometimes I will react to those losses with feelings of weakness and lessening, but sometimes there are better places I can get to.

In recent years, Marc was writing about deep space, and the facts he learned read like ideas described in the *Vedas*: solar systems and galaxies beyond number, time beyond all time-as-we-know-it, origin stories beyond our wildest imaginings. A friend said that vastness made him feel inconsequential; he didn't like to think about it. But I find it comforting because I am of that infinite, ineffable reality. I am of it at its largest scale and at its smallest scale. I am integral to it and couldn't leave its beauty even if I wanted to. India gave me the refuge of that perspective. Since the first time I read this story in the *Upanishads*, I've loved it, but I didn't *feel* it until I was in India. In the story, a dialogue occurs between a sage and his son, Svetaketu:

"Fetch me...a fruit of the *Nyagrodha* [banyan] tree."

"Here is one, Sir."

"Break it."

"It is broken, Sir."

"What do you see there?"

"These seeds, almost infinitesimal."

"Break one of them."

"It is broken, Sir."

"What do you see there?"

"Not anything, Sir."

"My son, that subtle essence which you do not perceive there, of that very essence this great *Nyagrodha* tree exists. Believe it my son. That which is the subtle essence, in it all that exists has its self. It is the True. It is the Self, and you, . . .Svetaketu, are it."

Lynn Litterine

John and David, Pennsylvania, September 1990

Acknowledgements

Marc Kaufman and Lea Chartock, for their generous and wise first readings of this manuscript

The late Carol Horner, for coming to share India with us, no matter what could happen

Diane Guidera McNicholas, for saving my letters from Delhi and sending them back to me for this book

Mrinal Mitra, for generously putting me, a complete stranger, in touch with the Children's Book Trust for copyright permissions

Navin Menon, publications editor of the Children's Book Trust, for giving me copyright permission to use its wonderful covers

David Litterine-Kaufman, for allowing me to quote from his journal

Gene Roberts, former executive editor of the *Inquirer*, for sending us to India on the newspaper's dime

My father, Louis Litterine, for keeping journals and letting me read them whenever I wanted to, and my mother, Elsa Holberg Litterine, for crafting so well the stories she told in our kitchen as she cooked

My girlfriends, for sharing with me a mad love of books, reading, and writing

The late Warren Shaffer, for introducing me to the magic I might find in literature if I dove deeply

Sven Birkerts, for his book *The Art of Time in Memoir: Then, Again*, a revelation to anyone interested in writing for others about their memories

And last but not least, my family—Marc, David, Angie, John, Beth, and Miles-- for the deep meaning they give my life

THE AUTHOR

Lynn Litterine was raised on the Hudson River across from 168th Street in New York. Her father was a plumber who kept journals off and on throughout his life. Her mother was home full time and told her great stories with beginnings, middles, and ends, usually while she cooked. She liked school, unless her teacher was scary. She quit college twice in the '60s then blundered into newspapers and found her home and her people at the *Hudson Dispatch*, the *Bergen Record*, and the *Philadelphia Inquirer*. She wrote and edited primarily for feature sections as they evolved from Women's World to Lifestyle. Her most memorable interviews were with two idols, Bette Davis and Allen Ginsberg. She married a journalist and had two sons. While they were young, she squeezed freelance writing in where she could. She finally got her BA from Bryn Mawr College at age 50 and then an MA in creative writing from Temple University two years later. She's taught writing at universities and for the federal government. As soon as she retired, she began writing creative nonfiction exclusively. Now she lives in Philadelphia for the fourth time; it seems to be home.